PARENTING FORWARD

Parenting Forward

How to Raise Children with Justice, Mercy, and Kindness

Cindy Wang Brandt

WILLIAM B. EERDMANS PUBLISHING COMPANY
GRAND RAPIDS, MICHIGAN

Wm. B. Eerdmans Publishing Co.
4035 Park East Court SE, Grand Rapids, Michigan 49546
www.eerdmans.com

Published 2019
Printed in the United States of America

25 24 23 22 21 20 19   2 3 4 5 6 7

ISBN 978-0-8028-7603-4

Library of Congress Cataloging-in-Publication Data

A catalog record for this book is available from the Library of Congress.

Contents

Foreword

As an author who writes about faith and justice, I am often asked during Q&A sessions how I plan to raise my kids to be good neighbors in an increasingly global neighborhood. For years I responded with long, considered answers, invoking everyone from Desmond Tutu to Mr. Rogers, citing Scripture, parenting philosophies, and the latest sociological studies as though I were an expert.

And then I actually had kids.

That's when, as so often happens, the reality of parenting came barreling through all my grand ideals about parenting, and suddenly I found myself—an accomplished career woman who doesn't think twice about speaking to audiences of thousands—sitting in the car sobbing after simply touring a preschool. I was totally and completely out of my depth. I knew how I *didn't* want to raise my two kids, but I wasn't sure how I *did* want to raise them.

Enter Cindy Wang Brandt.

Cindy is like that friend with an encyclopedic mind and an oversized address book. She doesn't know all the answers (who does when it comes to parenting?), but she knows someone else who has been through something similar, or she knows about a book that addresses this very issue, or she knows just the right tea and playlist for calming you down. Most importantly, she knows when to shut up, pull up a chair, and just listen.

Like so many others, I "met" Cindy through an online forum she curates for parents who want to raise their kids "unfundamentalist"—that is, without the fear, shame, and religion-based manipulation many Christian parents knew growing up. Forums like these can be difficult to manage, especially when they swell to many thousands of members as Cindy's has, but Cindy knows exactly how to spark, guide, and wrap up a conversation without being heavy-handed about it. She has a gift for turning these little corners of the Internet into virtual living rooms where people feel safe talking about their questions, their fears, their failures, and their hopes. Few endeavors trigger more insecurity than parenting, but Cindy sets the kind of tone that gives people permission to be honest, to vent, and to get help. I've learned so much from the collective wisdom of these groups through the years, and from Cindy specifically, I'm not sure I could ever calculate their impact on my life and on the lives of my kids.

This is why a book by Cindy is such a welcome treasure. In *Parenting Forward* the reader is treated to a robust and accessible guide to breaking the cycle of authoritarian, fear-based parenting in favor of a paradigm that pursues and celebrates equality, autonomy, and fully embodied health and wholeness, "one tiny act of love at a time, and moving on to the next small, right thing." In the pages ahead, you will encounter the Cindy whose mind is like a sponge, soaking in the wisdom of scientists, philosophers, and poets, and also the Cindy who is still figuring things out herself, modeling the sort of humility and openness for which she advocates in her own life as a parent, teacher, and friend. I recommend reading with a highlighter at the ready and a tissue box handy.

Much has been written in recent years about the benefits and drawbacks of our hyperconnected world. Certainly, there are days when I need to "unplug." But of the many gifts my Internet connection has provided, my friendship with Cindy has to be one of the most valuable. She has made me a better parent, a better Christian, and a better citizen of the world. There's not a doubt in my mind she will do the same for you.

Rachel Held Evans

author of *Searching for Sunday* and *Inspired*

I really love my job.

Shir, age 5

PARENTING FOR A BETTER WORLD

Dishes are an underdiscussed topic in parenting books. While others focus on children (not sure why that is), I feel like dishes deserve much more attention simply because of the amount of space they occupy in family life.

This morning, my child brought out six cups from his room. Six. If I've done nothing else right in parenting, I can be certain of this: I do a damn good job of hydrating my children. Nightly, I am overwhelmed by the enormous task before me as used plates and serving dishes await on the dinner table while piles of dirtied pots and pans and kitchen gadgets overflow the sink. It feels like an impossible job until it's done. Every Single Night. And how do I do it? I always start with the smallest dish, the one little measuring cup or the small sauce bowl. I scrub it, rinse it, place it on the drying rack, and move on to the next small thing.

Our world today feels like the disastrous kitchen after dinner, with messes, stains, and unknown substances caked on walls. As much as I am a progressive, believing the world improves human life over time, it's undeniable that we are facing some of the most severe crises history has ever seen. Our warming earth threatens us with record-breaking hurricanes, melting ice caps, and the annihilation of species. Social media gives us constant access to the pulse of societal ills, and we collectively feel the throbbing, rapid-fire beat of communities stressed from violence, strife, and tragedies. The news cycle relentlessly vies for our attention, mixing feelings of outrage and despair with no end or escape. Most of us react with instinctive fight-or-flight responses: either resisting every evil and finding ourselves in burnout, or succumbing to paralysis.

But there is another way. Overwhelmed with the bigness of the world's problems, we can start small. The small measuring cup, the small bowl, the smallest humans. The activists and celebrities are not the ones who effect change in the world. Or rather, I should say, they do it by exerting wide influence on all the ordinary people who are creating real change in their homes, around their dinner tables with their families.

This is how we build a better world: doing one tiny act of love at a time and moving on to the next small, right thing. Bit by bit, we can get the impossible job done by homing in on the small things with the small people.

Nelson Mandela famously said, "There can be no keener revelation of a society's soul than the way in which it treats its children." The children of our world form a window through which we find both the diagnosis and the cure for our sickness. They are first to feel the impacts of our various devastations. The ecological crisis, rampant consumerism and income inequality, violence and war disproportionately affect the littlest ones. According to UNICEF, nearly half of the world's extreme global poor are children, deprived of basic human rights such as nutrition, health, water, education, or shelter. And yet only half of the countries in the world even gather child poverty data.[1] When it comes to the world of development and humanitarian aid, it seems the old adage "Children are to be seen and not heard" applies— their cries for basic human dignity are largely ignored.

Naomi Klein, a world-renowned writer and activist on the issue of climate change, calls the current ecological crisis "intergenerational theft,"[2] robbing the next generation of a diversity of wildlife species, the wonder of the Great Barrier Reef, and a peaceful life free from the devastation of natural disasters as a direct consequence of a warming earth. Who bears the brunt of our poor stewardship? Children. We consume, they pay the debt—it is a grand theft of the most egregious kind.

The children in more privileged societies also suffer silently. From the bullied gay teen in public school to the five-year-old whose appetite to consume is being groomed by the billion-dollar advertising industry, from young Tamir Rice, shot fatally for playing with a toy gun, to girls who are catcalled, raped, and disbelieved—the way we treat our children is a grim diagnosis of the state of our moral consciousness.

But what if diagnosis is the first solid step toward a cure? What would happen if, instead of handing out domination, violence, manipulation, and hate, we treated children with generosity, gratitude, love, freedom, and peace? What if the solution to the world's complex problems begins in our homes and local communities, by unlearning the patterns with which we have treated children and having the courage to change? What if building a better world, a more just world, begins by raising one child— each child—with dignity?

The Long Game

We want results. Now. We want to solve problems, large and small, with hasty solutions. This short-term approach is the antithesis of the wisdom of every spiritual and philosophical tradition. Remember the hare and the tortoise? Slow and steady wins the race.

Coming up with solutions in the urgency of the moment, we often fail to listen deeply to those most affected by the crisis. In turn, our solutions don't account for the multilayered complexities of justice issues.

One well-documented example of Westerners rushing to "resolve" a water crisis in a poverty-laden region created a drill-and-run movement. According to reports, there are fifty thousand water supply points currently in disrepair across rural Africa.[3] Upon hearing the statistics, NGOs flooded into these regions, drilling wells to quickly alleviate the problem. Because they did not take the time to listen to the actual needs, narratives, and conventions of locals, they neglected the cultural dangers for women collecting water at the wells and failed to account for the financial sustainability of maintaining the wells beyond ten or fifteen years. Now these good-intentioned charity wells lie unused, deteriorating into disrepair. Up to $360 million was spent to drill and operate a shallow solution with no long-term impact.

For change to be real and meaningful, it almost always needs to be slow. This doesn't negate rapid progress in technology and advancements in all sectors of society that improve human lives. But it's one thing to possess high-speed tools for improvement and quite another to create personal and societal transformation. Changing minds and hearts in a way that is significant and long-lasting takes time. What better illustration for this than parenting a child?

Compared to other animals, human babies have a much longer maturation rate. A baby giraffe, for example, can begin to walk hours after birth, while humans require about a year to walk independently. And relative to our physical development, human cognitive development is even more prolonged. We now know, much to the relief and validation of parents of teens, that the prefrontal cortex of our brain does not fully develop until age twenty-five. This explains why teens aren't yet developmentally capable of making the most rational decisions.[4] But by the time we are fully developed, humans are capable of far more complex reasoning than any other species. It takes us longer to get there, but when we do, we have a remarkable capacity for complexity and growth.

In both parenting and building a better world, slow and steady wins the race. To accomplish the latter, we must invest in the former. To do justice well, we must commit to the long game of raising children *with* justice *for* justice.

Raising Children with Justice for Justice

Frederick Douglass wrote, "It is easier to build strong children than to repair broken men." His impassioned plea as an abolitionist from the 1850s has proved out the data. Recently, the Centers for Disease Control and Prevention, after collecting longitudinal data across 17,421 adults, concluded, "Childhood experiences, both positive and negative, have a tremendous impact on future violence victimization and perpetration, and lifelong health and opportunity."[5] The best prevention method for healthy adults and communities is investing in early childhood intervention. For every dollar spent on building strong children, we are saving much more in repairing dysfunctional adults.

According to the Costs of War project from Brown University, $4.79 trillion and counting have been spent on fighting the war against terror.[6] Still, the world doesn't feel significantly safer. A small Danish town called Aarhus is trying a different approach. A couple of police officers, Link and Aarslev, discovered young Muslim men in their town who were becoming radicalized by

ISIS recruiters. While neighboring countries in Europe treated young men who traveled to Syria harshly, since they were deemed at risk for engaging in terrorist activity, these two officers decided to be welcoming and kind. One particular story, reported by the NPR podcast *Invisibilia* for their series titled Flip the Script, involves a high school student, Jamal, who was on the verge of becoming radicalized from experiencing racial discrimination and marginalization in his school. When one of the officers, Link, gave this young man a call, his response was anger and aggression. Instead of meeting his aggression with more of it, the officer invited Jamal to his office and introduced him to a mentor, a fellow Muslim who experienced similar discrimination growing up but has been able to integrate into life in Denmark. Today, Jamal is following the same path and has abandoned any thought of radicalization.[7] "Flipping the script" from combating terrorism with violence to investing in mentoring young people is working. It could be significantly more cost-effective in ending the war on terror if we empowered young people to break cycles of racial, religious, and political discrimination.

The numbers inform a pragmatic understanding of doing justice to our children. But we are compelled not solely by data but by our own moral imperatives: our spiritual, religious, and moral obligation toward our children. In the Christian tradition, the basis for just treatment of children begins in the beginning chapters of the Bible, where humans are formed in the image of God and ac-

corded the highest value. In antiquity children were re-
garded as property, yet the biblical prophets repeatedly call
out for mercy for orphans, for justice for the marginalized
and vulnerable. In the New Testament, Jesus reprimands
his disciples for their conventional treatment of keeping
children away from the rabbi. In a radical move, Jesus the
rabbi welcomes the little children to come to him.

Throughout Scripture and history, God calls us to care
for the small, the oppressed, and the marginalized because
it is essential for every person's rising. Our flourishing
individually and as a society is closely linked to our treatment of the vulnerable.

Raising Ourselves

Parenting may be less about raising our children and more
about raising ourselves. As much as treating children justly
means respecting their human dignity, that just treatment
simultaneously strengthens our moral core. It compels us
to break our own cycles of shame and pain as we bring
needed healing to the wounds of our own childhood.

One Chinese proverb goes like this: Every family has a
scripture that's difficult to read. There is a story of struggle
in every household. Despite our Instagram-worthy family
pictures of smiles, imperfect humans living together inevitably hurt one another. The best parenting is done not in
the direction of our children but through the hard work
of deep healing within ourselves so that our children are

met with a healthy and whole parent imparting patterns of lovingkindness instead of shame.

In a heartrending blog post, writer Annie Reneau describes her father, who grew up with violence and alcoholism and yet donned a superhero cape by vowing to "give his children the childhood he didn't have."[8] He showed up for his children with love, laughter, and fresh hash browns on Sunday mornings. Despite failed moments, or rather human moments where he revealed the demons that haunted his past, he chose again and again to fight those demons. He was constantly doing the work of raising himself as he raised his children. This is bravery, because all of us are significantly affected by our upbringing, and parenting is largely instinctual.

I grew up with a lot of verbal shaming. A "good scolding" in my family and culture is considered acceptable and even a part of responsible parenting. As I grew into adulthood, I became aware of the negative impact that shaming words had on me. I believed the lies that I was unworthy. With my self-esteem cut through, it took a lot of self-affirmation and affirmation from friends and loved ones to overcome the harmful effect of those words.

When I had my own children, I swore to speak kind and gentle words to them, only to hear my parents' own harsh words slip through my lips, particularly in those moments of frustration. That chilling realization, *I sound just like my mother*, was a wake-up call that I must also work to raise myself. To learn to speak kind and gentle words to my children, I had to learn what I was not taught:

how to speak kind and gentle words to myself. By coming to terms with our own histories, we can break a cycle of dysfunction and boldly and beautifully step into a cycle of redemption. As our personal wounds begin to heal, we can push forward with a vision of peace, kindness, and justice for our children, who will grow into that vision and have a positive impact on the world.

This need for healing is as true for personal pain as it is for systemic, societal pain. Unless as parents we undergo the deep work of dismantling our own internalized racial, cultural, gender, economic, religious, and other biases, we will perpetuate and sustain those dysfunctions for future generations. But by becoming aware of our history and the complex ways we participate in systems of inequality or hierarchy, we begin raising ourselves to resist systemic injustice, we empower our children, and we change our communities.

Partnering with Children in Doing Justice

To do justice is to be in the business of subverting power. People, families, and systems that hold privilege and power over others are reluctant to let go of that power. Every revolution to grant equal rights to women, people of color, and sexual minorities involves costly resistance. One of the most effective strategies used by those who hold power to keep their power is to control the narrative. The saying "History is written by the victors" refers to the way those in power dictate the story, defining the struggle from their perspective. They ensure that reality is viewed through their lens, effectively silencing the voices of the marginalized. Therefore, the first essential component in our collective struggle for justice must be to un-silence, to give voice to those who have the greatest stake in the fight for equality.

Raising our children *with* justice *for* justice means making room for their voices. Children are to be seen and heard and invited to participate alongside us in our movements for justice. One illustration for this is Jenny Sowry's then twenty-two-month-old daughter: she held up a scrap of cardboard covered with crayon scribbles as a protest sign at the Women's March in Charlotte, North Carolina, in January 2017. Jenny explains that as she, her husband, and their nine-year-old son were working on signs for the protest, they noticed the toddler had taken to expressing herself with the crayons available to her. "We decided that she clearly had something to share and that whatever it was, it meant more to her than anything we might choose on her behalf." Sure enough, the little girl proudly held up her work at the protest. When a photo of her went viral, the internet bestowed on her the well-deserved title "Woke Baby."[9]

Some people balk at the idea of bringing young children to protests, claiming it is pushing adult agendas on children who have yet to determine their own causes. But children have historically been a part of the teaching and spreading of values alongside their parents, as at protests, notably in the civil rights movement.[10] It's a tangible way to demonstrate to children that they have a right and the power to influence the society they live in. What makes the parents of Woke Baby just as woke is that they gave their daughter her own voice, even when that "voice" looked like illegible doodles. Woke Baby is off to a hopeful start in life with parents instilling a strong sense of her autonomy of ideas. Building a strong foundation of self and reinforcing our intuition is what I call the Gospel according to Moana.[11]

The eponymous protagonist of the 2016 Disney animated film *Moana* is the daughter of the chief of a Polynesian village. The villain of the story is a mystical goddess called Te Fiti, who wreaks havoc on the region by upsetting the ecological balance, making life for the villagers unsustainable. Moana sets off on an adventure to find Te Fiti and restore the world to right. Along the way, she undergoes a hero's journey, and through the guidance of her wise, deceased grandmother who comes back to her through a vision, she learns to claim her identity as the girl who knows what she loves ("my island and . . . the sea"), who knows from whom she comes ("I am the daughter of the village chief . . . descended from voyagers"), who owns her past ("I am everything I've learned and more), but who knows where she is going ("come what may, I know the way, I am Moana!").[12]

With this newfound confidence and strength, she overcomes obstacles and finds her way to confront Te Fiti, who presents as a furious volcano oozing with angry hot lava. A Western, triumphalist, cowboy-saves-the-day ending would have Moana countering the angry goddess with greater power and kicking ass. But the surprising plot twist is that she confronts evil with lilting song.

> I have crossed the horizon to find you.
> I know your name.
> They have stolen the heart from inside you,
> but this does not define you.
> This is not who you are.
> I know who you are.[13]

It works. Te Fiti transforms from a destructive force into a beautiful, lush green island that provides abundantly for everyone within her ecosystem.

I grew up in a faith tradition with a theology of the "wretched soul." I was taught as a child that there was something irreparably damaged about me, that my own ideas were prone to be led astray and not to be trusted. This theology turned out to be toxic and served to diminish rather than affirm my selfhood. It also inhibited my capacity to love others more fully, calling those around me into their goodness. It's only when wholeness in oneself is shared for the wholeness of others that others move forward in love, courage, and trust. Life begets life. Developing a robust sense of self and identity, which is not an aspect of the wretched soul I was taught to believe in, is the truest way to become a selfless person.

This is the hard work we have to do, the healing work inside our own selves; this claiming of our individuality grounded in our community, both historically and geo-graphically; this inner work of forgiving our own past and forging onward. And through this work we will arrive at meeting our children's full humanity with a desire not to control them but to set them free.

In the first half of this book we will look at how to treat children with justice. How do we parent in such a way that our children are the most free? We are meant for integrity of being—our bodies, minds, and spiritual-ity make up the whole of who we are. Our main job as parents is to let our children unfold the beauty of their whole being as they grow. We will explore the posture of honoring their physical, imaginative, and spiritual au-tonomy by critiquing the ways society has sought to strip children of their rights and boundaries so that we can uncover our adult biases and offer them space to unfold into their unique selves.

Having built the foundation of treating children with gentleness, respect, and liberation, we will then move into the second half of the book and look at how to advocate for liberation of all. I offer concrete strategies for par-ents to equip our children to combat the injustices of our time: our ecological crisis, racism, homophobia, and sex-ism. These are by no means exhaustive strategies, and in the research for this book, I've discovered artists, activists, organizers who are constantly creating resources to expand our imagination for justice in the world. But what I do hope to do is draw our attention to the rich resource for justice we have in our homes and in the midst of our communities: the smallest among us, the children. Like the rest of us, they are both the beneficiaries and the agents of justice. Our work for justice will go much farther if we incorporate their voices and amplify the synergy from a multigenerational collaboration.

Sprinkled throughout the chapters I have included stories from my own upbringing, stories of parents and children, and stories from the news and history books. It is the stories of wild adventures that, just like the bedtime stories we tell our kids, empower us to live life. Let's make it good.

I asked Anders what, at six, he knows about God.
"Well," he said, "I know that God is loving.
That's all I know for sure so far."

Joy Neal, Anders's mom

1

A WHOLE GOSPEL
FOR A WHOLE CHILD

Krista Tippett, award-winning public radio host, begins all of her interviews with this question: "What is the spirituality of your childhood?" Whatever the subject of the interview, she has determined this to be the most revealing question that will provoke her guests to share of themselves with her audience. The spiritual landscape of our childhood harbors our deepest desires. It is where our vibrant imagination plays with the meaning of being human, which determines much of who we become in adulthood.

In my early childhood, my family was nonreligious. All I had available to me were some Chinese folklore picture books that described hell as eighteen levels of torture, depicted in graphic detail, which helped develop an existential angst in me. Enter the Christian missionaries who founded the school for missionary children that I was sent to. There I discovered a way to escape the tragic fate of eternal conscious torment. At the age of twelve I prayed what they called the "sinner's prayer" to secure my place with Jesus in heaven, thereby temporarily easing my anxiety about the afterlife. Little did I know that comfort came with spiritual baggage that kept me fractured for the rest of my childhood, and it has taken me the better part of my adult life to this point to try to piece myself back together.

The fire-and-brimstone salvation I was taught created a separation of our bodies and our souls, our right-now life and our afterlife. According to this split gospel, our bodies are a temporary vessel for the soul, which would be fetched back up to heaven when we meet our earthly demise. Alongside this incomplete gospel came authoritarian teachings that promoted literal readings of the Bible, hierarchies of control that kept women in submission to men, and a stance of fear toward liberals, science, people of different sexual orientations, other races, and other religions.

In high school I attended a short-term mission trip to Nepal, a nation ravaged by extreme poverty. I was still the same thoughtful, anxious kid, the one who contemplated the infinite future at six years old, so when I encountered the jarring reality of poverty, I asked that essential question that would later develop into a full-blown passion for social justice: *Why?* Why was I born into privilege and these people were born into poverty? It isn't fair! But I buried that curiosity about why within me because my spiritual environment taught me that while compassion for the poor was important, compassion for poor souls was more urgent.

It was a thin theology inadequate to express the realities I was experiencing. I remember meeting a woman who looked ancient, her skin wrinkled in a thousand folds, dark from a lifetime of labor in the sun. But she was only in her forties, and according to the average life expectancy for Nepalese at the time, she would die within a decade. As we, a group of wide-eyed youth, sang worship songs that spoke of salvation for our souls but not our bodies, I heard the silence of God. It was as if God had nothing to say about the life withering away from the Nepalese woman's overworked body.

At the Christian college I attended in the Midwest, I was part of a tiny minority of Asians in a sea of white students. At the time, I was grateful to be in a community of people who shared my faith and values. I believed we were equal members as brothers and sisters in Christ, working together for God's kingdom. Only later did I realize how much I had to minimize my own culture and experience of being Asian on a white campus. I later learned this was part of a process called "assimilation." I felt my race in my body as I moved about in the world, but this too was absent from conversations in my spiritual upbringing.

I have a trans brother, which means for our entire childhood I believed I had a sister because he was born in a female body and was raised as a girl. When he eventually embraced his trans identity and decided to undergo sex reassignment surgery, our family met with extreme resistance from our faith community. My brother was reprimanded for changing God's good, original design for his body. For me, this was a dramatic summary of the way my childhood religion sent conflicting messages regarding our bodies, which is that God and the gospel are mostly unconcerned with our bodies—except when it comes to matters of sex.

As I emerged into young adulthood to discover additional inconvenient truths, like global warming, and looked outward to the large-scale problems of global poverty and the war on terror, I was awakened to the truth that what we do in the present has consequences for God's creation here and now, as well as for our children and their children. At the same time, I had another awakening.

As I reflected on my own lived reality in my biologically female body, Asian olive skin, and within a patriarchal and white-supremacist system, I began to understand that for the gospel (which means "good news") to be truly good news for the world, it has to be concerned not just about spirituality but also about our bodies, our minds, and our politics. If the good news is to be good, it has to be good not just for a small demographic slice of the population but for people of all religions, ethnicities, sexual orientations, gender identities, economic statuses, and ages.

It felt like I had lived the first half of my life skimming the surface of all that my faith promised but failed to deliver. As I peeled away the layers, I discovered the possibility that a fuller faith could address what lies beneath: the richness of what the gospel has to say about our bodies, minds, and spirits and the ways they intertwine to make us an integral whole.

I became passionate about learning the political teachings within Christian tradition. I began to understand how Jesus challenged the power structures of his day with courage and to recognize that there was no separation of the spiritual and the political in his life. This kind of faith, I thought, had potential to be transformative for me and for the communities I inhabit—it could lead to real change, authentic growth, and a more just world.

I don't want my kids to have to live that fractured spirituality. I want to offer them the whole gospel, the good news that they can embrace an integrated view of themselves and engage authentically and fully with the world. But this is new territory for me personally, as a parent, and for the world, as human civilization is only beginning to recognize the need to offer children full autonomy.

The Evolution of Parenting

In the introduction, I said that parenting is largely instinctual. What I mean is that we are prone to repeat the patterns in which we were raised. As humans, we internalize the language and attitudes of our upbringing so that it becomes part of who we are. We are largely unaware of its presence, like the air we breathe—it just is. We mistake our natural parenting responses to be a universal instinct, somehow biologically wired to our being, when in reality parenting is extremely diverse and fluid.

I had my first baby in California, and my mother flew from Taiwan to be with me for the first month postpartum. It is a traditional Chinese ritual for the mother to take care of her daughter by helping out with the baby and feeding the new mother an assortment of Chinese herbal medicines to help with recovery. In that whirlwind month, I was receiving both the advice of Western pediatricians and my mother's wisdom from her own child-rearing days. The realms of advice were polar opposite. Lay the baby to sleep on her back in a crib away from your room, the doctors recommended. Strap the baby on you with a cloth and she can sleep while you cook, my mother quipped. Faced with conflicting information, I seriously questioned the idea of a maternal instinct: I honestly didn't know what was best for my baby.

Not only do parenting customs vary from night to day across cultures; they also vary significantly through time. Almost every modern parenting sensibility we have has developed only in very recent human history. Historians tell us that if you reach far back into early civilizations—appallingly—parents across the globe killed their young. And this wasn't done by savage men but by biological mothers who labored for their babies. Historian Lloyd deMause estimates that "millions of infant deaths can be attributed directly or indirectly to maternal tactics to mitigate the high cost of rearing them."[1] That's right, if any parental instinct is universal, it is infanticide. Although infanticide still occurs in some pockets of our world today, we have moved well beyond accepting violent brutalization of children as good parenting practice.

Clearly, parenting styles have evolved and progressed over the generations. Western historians date the ideal of a nurturing mother to the eighteenth century.[2] Since then, although parenting has become less vicious, dominion over children's autonomy continues to reign, albeit via subtler methods. Infanticide and abandonment morphed into severe corporal punishment in homes and schools, with the aim of controlling children. In the Industrial Age, children became cogs in the machine and child labor became accepted practice. Children were still treated as subhuman, and sex abuse was rampant. It wasn't until 1959 that the United Nations adopted the Declaration of the Rights of the Child, eleven years after the Universal Declaration of Human Rights, taking political steps to protect children from economic or sexual exploitation.[3]

In the past few decades, parenting styles have continued to evolve to be more kind to children, but physical violations of children's bodily autonomy have proven hard to overcome, and emotional and spiritual manipulation of children has taken root in insidious ways to keep adult power over children. Children can exist and have rights now, but they must be good compliant boys and girls, with parenting methods aimed at that goal.

Today, in the Information Age, the speed with which parenting styles progress has increased. We are at the cusp of a changeover to viewing children as full physical, emotional, and spiritual agents. It is becoming more clear that our job as parents isn't to shape our children into people who conveniently situate themselves in our world, but to afford them the liberty to grow into who they are. We are climbing the uphill battle to switch from an *authoritarian* to an *authoritative* mode of parenting.

Although parenting is instinctual and we are prone to repeat the patterns with which we are raised, the good news is that when we step back and view the larger picture of parenting history, we are not beholden to a biological mandate. We can evolve and push against harmful practices of the past and usher in a more beautiful vision of how to parent our children.

Good News for the Children

In the Christian fundamentalist parenting paradigm I grew up in, parents are tasked to bring up godly children via a top-down hierarchy. Armed with divine directives, parents act as agents of God to rule over children. Under this model, Scripture is used to justify spanking children into submission and physically coercing them into right behavior. This type of fundamentalism fails to create intrinsic motivations to do good and offers very little emotional validation because emotions are not to be trusted. A forced spiritual identity comes with a prescriptive list of behaviors with which the child must comply in order to fit the role of the good, godly kid. Add to that community expectations as external motivation for a child's moral behavior. None of this is good news for the child.

For those like me who see the way they were raised or their faith tradition as bringing harm to a child's personhood, what we are seeing in these years of parenting is this: a call to subvert the paradigm. Instead of the top-down hierarchy, we sow a foundation of love, connection, and justice toward children so that in their tender growing up years they can put down deep roots of physical security, emotional self-identity, and spiritual grounding to sustain a lifetime of living good and living well.

Our jobs as parents aren't to prescribe the kinds of fruit our children will grow but to be diligent in watering the roots of justice, letting each of their unique seeds germinate into their dynamic selves. Because of the inherent vulnerabilities of children, in order to topple hierarchy, we must be intentional in equalizing power dynamics between the adult and the child. This stands in stark contrast to an authoritarian parenting mindset, which fears a child who has power and control, believing children who have too much power will somehow drive themselves into being chaotic creatures and undermine parental authority.

Authoritarian parents seize control over their child and ensure power remains with the adult. This mistakenly assumes that respect is coerced instead of earned. On the contrary, the more we attempt to equalize power dynamics between us and our children, the more they gain the confidence and skills to navigate a give-and-take relationship with the parent. When we earn their trust, our influence over them is far greater than whatever values we impose on them, because they have been given the autonomy to choose it out of their own free will. Giving our power away, ironically, ends up bolstering our position of parental influence over our children's lives as we engage in mutual understanding and learning from one another. Our children raise us as much as we are raising them.

Dismantling Our Blind Spots

I have two children. When they were babies, one of them rarely cried, slept through the night, and ate well. The other required two night wakings to feed, fussed throughout the day, and was a picky eater. Conventional parenting vocabulary would have me call one child a "good" baby and the other a "bad" baby, or, to be less crass, an "easy" baby and a "difficult" baby. Thankfully, when they were little, I was introduced to the writing of Dr. Sears, a pediatrician and expert on attachment parenting, whose book *The Fussy Baby Book* taught me these terms instead: *low need* and *high need*.[4] The baby wasn't bad, I learned; he simply had needs he deserved to have met, and he wasn't going to let me get away with not tending to them. The way we speak matters, and it brings about a shift in a parent's attitude from feeling unlucky for having been given a "bad" baby to realizing that this baby is better at demanding the attention all babies need. Not only did this help me lessen resentment toward my high-need child;

it also helped me become more intentional in tending to my other child's needs. I realized she still needed my attention; she just didn't demand it.

Unsurprisingly, my high-need baby grew to be a highly sensitive toddler. He took his time speaking, but even before he was verbal, he would do or babble adorable things that elicited joyful delight from the adults around him. But we noticed that he would often startle at laughter that was directed at him, and often a tantrum would soon follow. Before he had the words to say, he was trying to tell us, "I don't like you laughing at me." Because of his needs, I began to become aware of how often adults respond to young children's antics with laughter. We do it because it's fun (for us) and such laughter is acceptable among adults, but we don't stop to consider how it affects the child. Certainly, some children perhaps aren't aware of being the subject of laughter, or even if they are, they do not mind. But what I appreciate about highly sensitive children, like my son, is that they boost the signal that something isn't quite right. They reveal the blind spots we may have as adults who have inherent power over children or the ways we do not treat children justly.

Would we laugh boisterously at other adults who said something when they weren't trying to be funny? Would we laugh even more when they objected to our laughing at them? That would be incredibly condescending, and yet this is what we do to children. Becoming aware of this reminds me that there are many ways we have yet to extend full equality and dignity to children in our world. We assume their concerns are not as legitimate as ours when we are in adult settings; we make jokes about how much alcohol we ingest just to take care of them all day long; we talk about them in front of them as if their opinions don't matter; we hit them; we manipulate them with our emotions; we punish them for being every bit as human as we are, just because we have the privilege of stature, resources, and experience.

Inevitably, when I bring up the injustice we commit against children, adults object. They either dismiss it as no big deal, or they assert the parent's right to have their needs met. And certainly, as mothers still bear a disproportionate burden of child-rearing in society, their physical and mental exhaustion in parenting requires catharsis and, more importantly, systemic support. But we must ensure that liberating women does not add to the oppression of children. The process of helping everyone rise may be complicated and imperfect, but we have to strive for equality for all and nothing less. The nature of privilege is that we've internalized it to be normal, and the only way to dismantle it is to be open to having our blind spots exposed.

This is the good work of parenting: to listen to the voices of the children telling us when we are being unjust; to avoid waiting until their woundedness follows them into adulthood before breaking the cycle. We are children as well, in adult versions, who bear the hurt of being treated as "less than" when we were children. As child development experts have continued discovering what is best for the child, we have the tools, the means, and the understanding to do better. Parenting forward is imagining what isn't reality yet and striving for it, daring to believe it's possible for both the parent's needs and the child's needs to be fully met, and for equality and justice to finally be available to all children.

There's a reason why, when my son who's six is crying, he needs a hug. It's not just that he needs my love. He needs a boundary around his experience. He needs to know that the pain is contained and can be housed and it won't be limiting his whole being. He gets a hug and he drops into his body.

Matthew Sanford,
*Waking: A Memoir of
Trauma and Transcendence*

2

GOOD NEWS
FOR THE BODY

It takes a toddler five to seven seconds to express glee. I'm not sure what it is—perhaps facial muscles in young children are still developing—but it literally takes that long for them to arrange their features into excitement. First, their little mouths slowly morph from an "ooh" to an "oh" to a wide open "ah," and then their tiny nostrils flare ever so slightly. Mid-nostril-flaring, their eyes begin to shine with a sparkle and widen as if the size of their eyes determines the amount of pleasure they can take in. Lastly, as the climactic finale, their eyebrows rise so high it shifts the hairline, and with that, without yet uttering a single sound, their countenance screams: I am happy.

Our children enter this world as fully embodied beings. Babies arch their backs as they exercise their vocals to cry for milk and for love. They kick their legs for joy, reach out their arms for attention, and blow raspberries for sport. They put apples in their mouths as well as their favorite board book, as if there's no difference between satiating hunger for the body and the mind. While adults learn a certain degree of social filter, children speak with unabashed honesty, giving direct access from the thoughts in their brains to the world. Their inner and outer lives are integrated: what you see is what you get. As adults we mostly delight in this (exceptions taken for when you are the target of a child's brutal public observation), because that sense of wholeness is refreshing. Children remind us what we have given up, because somewhere along the way we had to sever those connections between our bodies and our minds and begin living in a disintegrated way. Each time we were reprimanded for our screams in the grocery aisle or shamed by the looks of strangers, we learned we had to stifle our voice. We learned that even though it hurts inside, we cannot let it show.

When we leisurely savored each morsel of our food on the tray, we were rushed to finish our meal so that we learned pleasure came with time limits. When we skipped, ran, and jumped with abandon, we were cautioned to be careful so that we learned our bodies were fragile, inadequate for the energies inside of us. We began to be taught what size our bodies had to be: girls had to be small, boys had to take up space. Racial inequalities ranked us according to the shade of our skin. Our gender expression had to match our genitalia or we risked severe bullying. So we gave our bodies over to the world, letting them conform more and more to what is acceptable while watching them drift away from who we really are. We severed ourselves from our bodies and became accustomed to compartmentalizing various aspects of our identity.

As parents, our first task is to raise ourselves and learn to welcome our bodies back in alignment with our minds and spirits. When we do, we create a better world in which our children aren't forced to divorce their minds and spirits from their bodies. The Christian gospel I discovered in my early adult world is one in which the Word became flesh: an embodied existence of the divine and the human body. The good news for our children is one that includes their body as a beautiful integration into their being, not a severing. I've been asked if I think Jesus the toddler ever threw a tantrum. Can a perfect God and the epitome of human standards have a meltdown in aisle 7 of Target? I have to believe the answer is a resounding yes because a toddler tantrum isn't imperfection but the normal human process through which we learn to regulate our emotions. At two years old, we flail our arms and legs and throw ourselves onto the floor, and given holistic guidance, we emerge from that stage with maturing sensibilities that lean into our bodies instead of away from them.

Instead of requiring that our children detach themselves from the ways their bodies reflect their being, we give them the space and time to make peace with their bodies, honoring them, building a secure self-identity within them. Serena Williams, the professional tennis player, speaks a message to her newborn daughter in a 2017 Gatorade commercial titled "Sisters in Sweat."[1] Through sports, she says, "you'll discover the power and grace of your body. You'll learn to move, and you'll learn the way to move others." When our children learn to be in right relationship with their bodies, they'll move and move others.

When Touch Honors Consent

Our children are a product of the physical intimacy we have with our partners, and they are delivered through yet another physically intense and mystical process, that of labor. Our physical relationship with our children begins before they even arrive and continues when they are born. That relationship has the power to transform our children for their flourishing or for trauma. A newborn is consumed with meeting his physical needs—to be fed, changed, and held. The way we respond to that need, bringing his skin into direct contact with ours on demand, fills his bucket so that he is ready for his next developmental stage of independence.

Justice for a baby is upholding her human right to be touched as often as she needs, which is determined by her cues in communication with her bonding partner. Studies are clear: frequent skin-to-skin contact increases a baby's well-being with better physical health (cardiorespiratory stability), mental health (optimal brain development and decreased crying), and social connection (deeper bonding and attachment).[2] The touch that we offer, generously without reservation in those early days, contributes to a baby falling into alignment with her body. When her need for touch is fulfilled, it gives her life.

A baby filled up with security in knowing his cries are met with loving touch will eventually grow into a toddler with newfound physical capabilities to begin exploring his world. This is often when parents begin to fear the child's independence will assert itself, when the child has the will to become defiant against their expectations. From reasons as benign as protecting a toddler's safety to toxic religious teaching, parents feel the pressure to dominate physically over the small child with corporal punishment.

There is no better way to exile a child's mind and spirit from her body than to inflict pain at the hands of someone who is supposed to care for her. Many parents make the distinction between physical abuse and spanking, which they consider a controlled instrument that leads to a desirable outcome. Rest assured, a young child does not see it that way. In a study conducted in the UK of seventy-six children from the ages of five to seven, the children reported the spankings they received with phrases like "someone banged you with a hammer," "breaking your bones," and "when you're in the sky and you're falling to the ground and you just hurt yourself."[3] In her acceptance speech for a peace award in West Germany, Astrid Lindgren, author of *Pippi Longstocking*, told a story of a mother who asked her son to go outside to find a switch for a spanking. After a while, the son came back inside not with a switch but a rock. Crying, he said, "I couldn't find a switch, but here's a rock you can throw at me."[4] From a child's perspective, there is no difference between a light tap and physical abuse. Violence is violence. Not only does decades of research prove that spanking does not work, in that it is not effective in changing a child's behavior in the parent's favor;[5] spanking also leads to plenty of undesired results, including increased aggression, antisocial behavior, physical injury, and mental health problems.[6]

Although spanking is still culturally acceptable in most of the world, the anti-spanking movement is spreading. In 2017, Scotland joined more than fifty countries in banning parents from spanking children, the first country in the UK to do so. One of the main opponents to this law, however, is an organization named Christian Institute, which heavily funded the pro-spanking lobbying in the name of the "truths of historic, biblical Christianity."[7] Indeed, much of the support for continuing corporal punishment comes from religious fundamentalists.

When religion is used to enforce authoritarian teaching, it results in damaging children's bodies. Fundamentalist Christian parenting literature often instructs parents to have a talk with their children before or after spanking, explaining that the violence they are about to inflict is for the children's sake, to restore them back to God, and that this act is done in love. It takes cognitive dissonance for a child to translate physical pain as emotional love (not to mention the toxic theology that preaches a God who aims to hurt a child). This kind of spiritual manipulation places a wedge between children's physical bodies and their intuitive sensibilities. They have to divorce their bodily feelings from their emotional and spiritual selves in order to maintain the worldview their parents are teaching—for how can love feel like violence?

Good news for children's bodies is that our touch is always offered to express our love. How we connect to their bodies should be consistent with the love we speak into their hearts and the theology we preach to their souls. Our touch should protect, soothe, comfort, delight, play with, and love our children; it should never inflict pain.

The root of corporal punishment is the will to dominate a child, using physical force to manipulate a child into adult-preferred behavior. When it becomes socially and culturally unacceptable to spank, parents may change their discipline practices, but the desire to dominate a child will adapt into subtle forms of physical aggression or emotional manipulation. We have to address the fundamental shift required to move from domination to liberation. What does emancipation of children's bodies look like? Is it enough to simply stop assaulting their bodies? Certainly, that is a crucial change and one in which we must continue the momentum in turning the societal tide, but the paradigm change to release our power over children will manifest in the transformation of myriad parenting practices.

The opposite of dominion is building a strong and steady current that supports a child's agency over her own body. We want our children to confidently proclaim, "My body is my body. It belongs to me." This runs counter to the truncated theology of my youth. I can still recite the memory verse from my little Navigators brown leather pouch, Romans 12:1, "Therefore, I urge you, brothers and sisters, in view of God's mercy, to offer your bodies as a living sacrifice, holy and pleasing to God—this is your true and proper worship" (NIV). As a child, I took this to mean my body did not belong to me, that it belonged to God instead. I was fortunate in not encountering sexual predators who twist the meaning of such Bible verses to manipulate children. But the same cannot be said for the many children who have been physically and sexually abused by religious leaders who took advantage of children's vulnerability.

The molestation of children by Catholic priests has been well documented. In recent years Boz Tchividjian, the grandson of Billy Graham, has labored to raise awareness that the problem of child abuse in Protestant churches is just as alarming, citing the church as the ideal environment for sexual predators to target children.[8] Tchividjian founded GRACE (Godly Response to Abuse in the Christian Environment), which helps train churches to institute effective child abuse prevention policies to keep children safe. These policies and safeguards are vital, and parents can support this work by helping children hone their radars against violations to their bodies, to be able to trust themselves when the warning signals are blaring in their intuition that something is off.

I hated being tickled. The worst part about tickling is that the body involuntarily laughs in response so that it communicates a message of delight. I have no doubt some children enjoy being tickled, and if so, they will en-

thusiastically invite it. But as a child I got terribly fright-
ened when I was tickled to the point of not being able
to breathe and, worse, when I begged my tickler to stop
and they wouldn't. For the most part, adults or persons of
power over a child are not trying to hurt a child by tickling
them; it is a playful act. However, it is play at the expense
of a child unless the child gives consent to be part of the
game. Pre-puberty, we can begin teaching children that
they have agency over their bodies by not engaging in
play that dominates their bodies without their consent.
Always stop when they ask for a game to end. Same goes
for hugs and kisses and wrestling and snuggles. As soon
as children begin to sense their bodies are a separate entity
from others, we can respect that boundary. Some children
are going to be more physically affectionate than others,
just as adults vary in the degree of touch they prefer. Read
their cues and let them determine how much physical
touch they want from you, because love without boundaries can veer dangerously into abuse. "My body is my
body. It belongs to me."

Agency in Clothing and Food

When we think of the most basic responsibilities of parents, we think of clothing and feeding children. These
tasks have an intimate relationship to children's bodies.
Clothing is the fabric that lies directly against a child's
skin, the largest organ of our body, providing not just func-

tional warmth but a poignant way through which a child expresses his identity. If you look at the diversity of clothing across cultures, it becomes clear that clothing is largely a social construct and only minimally an implement for survival. We are all born into and bound by culture, and there's no need to deny that we inevitably envelop our children in our culture.

But do we want to raise children who fall into line with what culture imposes on them, or do we want our children to grow into culture creators and makers? To accomplish the latter, we can cultivate their agency in what they put on to clothe their bodies. Their ability to create is predicated on their freedom. This is a dance, because parents are the ones who spend their money buying clothing, and we may have choices of our own that we want to honor. For example, perhaps we choose not to buy from brands that are exploitative of child labor, or we only purchase secondhand from Goodwill out of respect for the environment. But children also have choices, and within the restraints of respecting the boundaries of both parent and child, we can give children as much freedom as possible in making and consenting to clothing choices. If we are honest with ourselves, the way our children dress presents the image we want to give to the public. Perhaps we've always dreamed of dolling up our girls in frilly dresses or putting a cute bow tie on our boys. Or we want to show off our wealth or status by having our children dress in name brands or fashionable styles. These speak more about the parents' image than about the child's agency, when the real concern is in attending to the latter. What does it matter to gain the world's approval if our child breaks inside? Within reason, let your child dress the way they choose; it will go a long way in reinforcing their creativity and personal style, which will lead to confidence in other areas of life. Really, it's okay! Spiderman jammies paired with rainbow tutus is the whimsy we all need.

Food is the love language of every Chinese family. Feeding one's child is the primary way a parent shows love, and that is a beautiful thing. In Chinese preschool, my son's teachers would spoon-feed him every last bite of rice and other dishes, whereas my own Westernized parenting preferences encouraged his independent feeding abilities. Food is another one of these big subjects where values, practices, and bodily agency intersect. Some frugal parents are understandably concerned about food waste, for both economic and environmental reasons, and expect their children to finish every last morsel. Others are health conscious or subscribe to religious diets and prepare their family meals accordingly. It's important to honor each family member's preferences and to take into account the child's agency. Ingesting food affects not just one's physical well-being but also one's emotional and even spiritual well-being. Unhealthy individuals often "eat their feelings" by using food as a substitute for unmet needs. Many religious practices include periods of food deprivation in order to increase devotion. Building a solid foundation for a healthy relationship between a child and her food is vital to a lifetime of well-being.

In the conversation about consent, the central issue is always power. How can we give our children power over what they eat? Can we give them choices? Can we include them in the process of food preparation? Can we, within reasonable limits, allow them to reject certain foods just because it's their preference? This too is cultivating children's agency in that they get to decide what goes inside their bodies.

My friend Iris Chen writes in her blog *Untigering* that she does not limit her boys' eating and snacking habits.[9] She allows them to eat whatever is in the house, including all the unhealthy junk food. She asks us to imagine what it would be like to be offered a buffet every single day. At first we may gorge on all of the foods, but sooner or later we will probably begin to self-regulate and become aware that crossing certain boundaries leads to feeling ill or dissatisfied. By releasing strict parental control, Iris is giving her boys the opportunity to get to know their own bodies—what makes them full, what makes them happy, what feels good at the moment but later makes you crash. Since giving them this freedom in their choice of diet, Iris has noticed that the boys have increased self-control, fewer power struggles, and more developed critical thinking skills. She says, "Sooner or later, our kids will have access to the king of all buffets: adulthood."

Children who have not been given the opportunity to practice self-control will struggle to cope with the choices available to them in adulthood. Giving our children autonomy over food early on will help build their gauges for their own bodies, giving them control and power over how they feel desire and feel fulfilled. If food is love, then the best way to feed our children is for them to voluntarily accept what's freely offered to them. Nobody wants to be spoon-fed love.

Sexual Agency

Of course, our bodies crave more than biological sustenance. We are also sexual beings. There's a good reason parents squirm when it comes to talk of the birds and the bees, one of the most mysterious, ecstatic, and also controversial topics in parenting.

I chuckle when I recall the *VeggieTales* rendition of the biblical story of David and Bathsheba, a story about lust, adultery, and murder. I had thought to myself, How are they going to make this story child-friendly? It turns out they made David a cucumber and Bathsheba a rubber ducky. Even though King David can have all the rubber duckies he very well pleases, he wants one particular rubber ducky and he steals it from a "poor man." Although it is offensive to me that a woman be compared to a literal object, a rubber ducky, it is actually not far from the truth regarding the worth of women in King David's time. Nevertheless, it is time we do better in having conversations about sex and sexuality with our children. Certainly, we can move beyond euphemisms to shape the narrative around our children's bodies, sexual pleasure, and sexual ethics.

The first thing to consider doing is to deconstruct the notion of the "sex talk" with kids—to expand the conversation on sexuality to a much broader scope over a longer period of our child-rearing years. Sex is so much more than intercourse: it's about pleasure, vulnerability, relationships, and love. To go back to my earlier example of tickling sessions, way before a child reaches sexual maturity, we are already teaching her much about how her body can feel pleasure, that pleasure can lead to joy and delight, but that you can at once feel pleasure and then want the sensation to end. If we want our children to grow into having healthy, reciprocal sexual relationships, then we want to begin their lives by building a strong sense of understanding their self-pleasure. Every person experiences bodily pleasure differently; this is why some kids love to be tickled and others, like me as a child, do not. We learn to hold our babies a certain way, hug them with a certain amount of pressure, always making sure we are learning and respecting their bodily sensations.

Exploration of their own bodies is a primary way through which children learn what makes them feel pleasure. But cultural, community, and religious shame and stigma surrounding genital self-stimulation sends the message that pleasure is wrong or even sinful, that our bodies can't be trusted to tell us what is good for ourselves. This too is a harmful disintegration to a child's holistic sense of self. Babies reach into their diapers and toddlers tug at their penis long before it is a sexual act. Like other areas of parenting, we can provide gentle guidance in social boundaries and decide together what is acceptable to each family member's comfort levels, while giving our children the opportunity and freedom to touch themselves without shame. This lays a firm foundation so that they remain connected to their bodies as they grow into puberty and sexual maturity.

Our conversations on sex are incomplete, however, if we speak only of bodily pleasure. A healthy sex life includes generously giving oneself to another while maintaining secure boundaries and self-identity. As Bromleigh McCleneghan says in her book *Good Christian Sex*, the gravest sexual sin isn't pleasure but "a lack of mutuality, reciprocity, and love."[10] The "sex talk" falls under the much larger umbrella of parenting our children in relationships in general.

Teaching our children healthy sexuality includes showing them what it means to be intimate, first with their primary caregivers, then, as their world expands, with their peers, and eventually with sexual partners. Instead of drawing a hard stance—no sex before marriage—and working backward to institute regulations with our teenagers to avoid breaking the ultimate rule, what teaches better is proactively modeling healthy intimacy from birth and ushering our children into a sexual ethic as they come of age. The business of risking ourselves in love begins when we birth our children, when we suddenly find our hearts walking in the wild of this world. It begins when we hold our babies, feed them, change their diapers, and get to know their different cries, their rhythm of sleep, their favorite foods. Moment by moment in our family lives, we are showing them what it means to know and be known, to love and be loved. And as we foster their relationship skills with siblings, grandparents, and their own peers, teaching tools of conflict resolution and guiding them to be generous and kind while drawing important self-care boundaries, we contribute to their ability to know their own emotions and how to manage and offer them in tender vulnerability. Sexuality is inextricably linked to emotional intimacy.

Toxic masculinity and femininity sever the connection between our body and mind. Toby Morris, a cartoonist from Auckland, New Zealand, who went to an all-boys high school, had this to say about that environment: "The culture was competitive, dog-eat-dog. You mock or get mocked. And with no women around, a really narrow, monolithic, version of how to be a man was all there was. 'Rugged' was the word when I was there. Staunch. No weakness. You know the plan, go do it: Get rich. Sink piss. Score chicks. DOMINATE." Sex, he says, was about personal conquest, involving metaphorical language such as "score," "on the prowl," and "wingman."[11] In this view, for boys and men sex is what your body does to another body, scoring and dominating, devoid of emotional intimacy. Girls and women, on the other hand, are told from magazine covers and ads that their bodies are to be consumed as products and objects of pleasure for men; who they are matters less than what size they are and how desirable their body is. Therefore, good news for the body is to address the toxic masculinity and femininity in our world so our children can grow into men and women restored to their bodies.

When we reclaim the sanctity and integrity of our bodies as active agents, we can engage with the world fully in our embodied selves. Witnessing the development of our children can be so captivating because their growth is so riveting and predictably unpredictable. I remember how, when my kids were little, my husband and I would wake up one morning, go to the crib, and look at different babies because they would seemingly have changed overnight. Next thing we knew, we were waking up to toddlers spouting new words or preteens sporting new attitudes that would just pop up with no warnings. The rapid changes in their bodies projected the tumultuous changes taking place internally. When we honor the way our children's bodies take up space in this world, we respect their bodies for the holy work that they do: creating meaning, belonging, and art with their dynamic selves.

Lessons of God

Lesson #1: God is always knocking on the door of our hearts and will never force his way in but will wait patiently for us to choose to open the door.

Lesson #2: God is blowing never-ending bubbles of love toward us and will keep blowing them even if we pop them.

Noah, age 7

3

PARENTING
FOR IMAGINATION

A day before popular artist Beyoncé appeared at the half-time show of the 2016 Super Bowl, she released a new song and music video called "Formation." It exploded onto the pop-culture scene, inspiring think pieces unpacking the layers of meaning delivered by the charismatic black star. In this stunning and provocative video, Beyoncé boldly displays her black identity and unsubtly points her (middle) finger at those who do nothing to relieve the modern struggles and injustices the black community faces. As she lies on top of a police car sinking into the waters, alluding to both the tragic flooding from Hurricane Katrina and police brutality against black bodies, the scene cuts to a young boy dancing in front of a lineup of an all-white police riot squad. His mesmerizing movement infuses vibrant life into his dynamic body while the police stand expressionless and flat. At the end of his dance routine, he emphatically stomps his foot into a stance and majestically stretches out his small arms. On that simple but powerful cue, the police uniformly raise their hands up into the air

as if surrendering to this black boy. This enactment of social reality performed in dramatic reversal transfers power
from the weaponized police squad to a single, vulnerable
boy with black skin. And the audience is called to confront the realities of unarmed black boys killed by police.

This transfer of power from the strong to the weak,
in particular to children, is a consistent part of biblical
narratives. In the Old Testament, God uplifts children
and calls them into sacred vocations, like Jeremiah the
prophet. "Don't say, 'I'm only a boy,'" the voice of God
encourages him (Jer. 1:4–10 *The Message*). If you follow
Christian parenting literature, you'd be led to believe that
good Christian kids must obey parents, when in reality the
Bible itself is full of dissenting children. Ezekiel 20:18–19
teaches this, "Don't do what your parents did. Don't take
up their practices" (*The Message*). Jesus himself defied his
parents as a child, sneaking away without their knowledge. When they found him at the temple, his mother
scolded him by saying, "Son, why have you treated us like
this? Your father and I have been anxiously searching for
you" (NIV). At which point Jesus committed the ultimate
bad-Christian-kid misdemeanor: he talked back (Luke
2:41–52).

For too long, the religious and cultural imperative
for children was to obey. Families, schools, and churches
worked with the following framework: "Children are like
empty buckets; they grow by being filled with whatever
we pour into the buckets." This unidirectional way of
engaging children—hierarchical, top-down, authoritar-

ian—robs children of a basic human right, the right to think their own thoughts. An extreme and yet popular teaching among Christian parenting leaders is what they call "first-time obedience." It demands nothing less than the child obeying the parent the first time a parent speaks. This model allows no room for negotiation and no empathy toward a child's autonomy; it is a hundred percent parental authority and zero percent a child's voice. I have seen family friends who have raised their children this way and it works: they are compliant and sweet and . . . invisible. First-time obedience erases a child's will and violates his right to speak and to push against boundaries, and worst of all, it steals his imagination. When children are commanded to conform to parental directives, what need is there for them to think for themselves?

As a young adult, I remember feeling stumped by simple questions like "What flavor of ice cream do you want?" or "What's your favorite color?" Ironically, I managed to choose a marriage partner at twenty-two years of age and yet could not for the life of me decide on a color for the bridesmaid dresses. I began to realize that many life choices, both small and large, had been made by my parents and other authority figures in charge of me. All I had to do was obey. I was never consulted on these sorts of decisions in my childhood. I learned how to obey in life, but it did not prepare me well for life.

It has been a painstaking journey of many years as I have dug deeply into myself to excavate my own desires and begin to trust my own choices. This isn't an uncommon experience for people my age. Many refer to the twenties and thirties as the time of life when you get to know who you are and own it. To a certain extent I agree that it takes years of trying new things and having experiences to know what you like and dislike, but what if this process can begin much, much earlier?

As parents, we make decisions for our kids often because, well, they don't know better. We can't just let them eat however much ice cream they want—they'll eat whole pints at one sitting and get sick! They don't know better. We can't let them play in the snow without mittens— they'll get frostbite! They don't know better. But what if we assume they don't know better because when we were kids, we were never trusted by our parents to know better?

We underestimate how much children know. Or, at least, we underestimate how much they have the capacity to learn if given the opportunity. We have some advantages over them in knowledge and experience, but they have the benefit of fresh perspective and vibrant imagination over us. They have just as much to teach us as we do to teach them. We honor that and strengthen their own intuition by soliciting their opinions as often as possible and by giving them opportunities to practice self-examination to determine their desires, interests, and beliefs.

Helpful parenting advice for dealing with tantruming toddlers is to give them a choice. Instead of saying "No, you can't wear this," ask "Would you like to wear the red shirt or the blue shirt?" This minimizes frustration because the adult in power is passing the power to the child, equalizing the dynamic in the interaction. Little by little, the child begins to learn about herself—whether she prefers the red or the blue shirt, the flavor of ice cream she likes, and which genre of books she most enjoys—and she builds her own repertoire of traits that make her who she is. What we do when we reinforce children's preferences is to give them tools to become self-aware of who they are and to have the freedom to live that out.

As children grow in their cognitive capabilities, one of the best questions parents can ask is "What do you think?" This is an underappreciated power phrase. To take seriously children's opinions is to honor them as full human beings, giving them the dignity of contributing meaningfully to conversations. Respecting children's thoughts empowers them to believe their voices matter, their ideas matter, and ultimately that they matter. They deserve to be fully present to take up space in our world despite their small stature and young age. And their ideas, when children are given the chance to present them, will enrich our lives in ways we have yet to see.

The newly elected prime minister of New Zealand, Jacinda Ardern, was giving a speech in Parliament when a group of school children walked in, at which point she stopped her speech to welcome them. Smiling and gesturing with her arms for the children to come to the front, she asked the politicians in the room, "No one minds if the next generation joins us for a moment?"[1] More and more we must integrate the presence of children into spaces that have historically been deemed too solemn, too reverent, and too important for children, experimenting with whether their spontaneity and noise is as disruptive as we fear, or whether perhaps, instead of detracting from adult spaces, they actually add their energy and imagination to expand adult paradigms.

My friend Anna Skates, a former children's director at a church, is experimenting with an intentional faith community named Imaginarium in Nashville, Tennessee. One of the goals for the community is to be truly multigenerational, which means that from the brainstorming stage of this project they involved kids' voices. They asked children the "What do you think?" question to gather their input on what an intentional community might look like. To help put adults at ease during this experimental process, Anna produced several short videos with the hashtag #ThisMightHappen, featuring children who are awkwardly silent and others who are endlessly chatty, to remind us that children don't abide by adult social conventions. "At Imaginarium, this might happen, and that's okay!" Anna says, winking and smiling. She has adopted the beautifully disarming role of bridge builder to help ensure the success of their dream: to build a place where all are truly welcome.

Creative Agents

Extending children the autonomy to think for themselves is not just a safeguard for their human rights and dignity;

it also opens the door for their imaginations to flourish. For my entire childhood and beyond, I never believed I was "the creative type." Somehow I was led to believe that to be a creative person I had to be good at singing and dancing, or drawing and painting. Worse, I thought that you had to be a certain type of person and that only a small segment of the human population was that type. Today I work as a creative person, writing and crafting words. But to get there, I first had to discover that I deserved to take up space in the arena with my voice. I realized that simply by owning my personhood, my worth, and my existence in this world, I could have an impact that moves other people and changes the shape of history. When I speak, via the words typed on my keyboard, I am making art full of beauty and truth that connects me with others.

We are all creatives. Every human brings their unique perspective and creates beauty in the world that did not previously exist. And, yes, this includes every child. The children in our lives are creative beings. This doesn't mean their art isn't still rudimentary and that diligence and time aren't required for honing their individual crafts, but these things don't diminish their creative essence, their right to be creatives by virtue of being human. This is the core of the good news that I discovered and recovered: we all are made in the image of a creative God, born to imprint our art on the world in our unique way as we move through life.

Brad Montague, creator of the popular web series Kid President, smuggled children's art into the Guggenheim.[2] He and his team had asked kids to submit their art depicting what it means to have hope. They packed up the submissions into a cardboard tube, tucked it inside Brad's overcoat, and smuggled hope into the museum in Manhattan, New York, a museum housing some of the best art from around the world. There they displayed every piece of scratch paper with the children's doodles so that every kid could say they had art appear in the Guggenheim. Among the kids was nine-year-old Safeen, an Iraqi refugee, who drew a picture with the caption "Hope is learning English so I can read to my little brother." Imagination births art and gives rise to hope, and hope belongs to every child.

A parent shared with my online community the way his kid plays with a nativity set from his conservative grandparents. "He's declared that the stable is a farmer's market, Joseph is a woman named Rar-rar, and Mary's name is now Celebrate. Mostly they fall down and help each other get back up." This kid isn't playing by rules. No religious system is keeping him from being irreverent with holy figures. No social construct of marriage and gender deters him from being a nonconformist in his play. And this lack of structure and chaos is leading him to kindness: his figures help each other get back up when they fall. For children, being human is about using their imaginations and having the freedom to play with their ideas, thoughts, and emotions.

Imagination is also the vital way through which children learn and cope with the struggles of life. Imagining potential outcomes empowers children to fight the battles that rage within and without. Children's literature doesn't merely transport children into the land of magic; it transfers the magic from the pages of the book back into their reality. Jerry Griswold, in his book *Feeling Like a Kid: Childhood and Children's Literature*, says, "Kids think through their problems by creating fantasy worlds in ways adults don't. . . . Within these parallel universes, things can be solved, shaped and understood."[3] Children work through their anxieties by reenacting scenarios in fantasy. When a villain meets his demise at the end of a plot line, monsters that haunt children in real life are also defeated.

Often children who are particularly imaginative are the most anxiety-ridden kids, because they conjure up a million scenarios in which things can end badly for them. Psychologist Eileen Kennedy-Moore suggests that instead of offering reassurances that none of those worst-case scenarios will take place (which we cannot guarantee), we should encourage children to use their imaginations to expand possibilities beyond their nightmares. She uses the example of a kid who worries that others will make fun of her because of her haircut. The parent can encourage her to imagine alternatives, offering suggestions like "What if they don't notice your haircut?" or "What if they say, 'Oh, you got a haircut,' but they're not very interested, so then they just keep doing what they were doing?" or "What if they say, 'Nice haircut,' and then just keep doing what they were doing?"[4] A child who is capable of imagining worst-case scenarios can also imagine alternatives; the imagination that dooms her is also what will save her.

There is a gaping generational chasm that I have not managed to cross: the phenomenon of *Minecraft* You-Tube channels. Essentially, they are screenplays of people playing their video games. I suppose it's the modern equivalent of me as a kid loitering behind other people playing video games in arcades because I didn't want to spend my own dime. My children love tuning into these channels. A while back I gently suggested they consider making these videos themselves. After I gave them a quick video-editing tutorial, they were ready to set up their own YouTube channel. If you hop on over to their channel, OmegaSound, you too can join all of nineteen other subscribers—it is clearly the latest trend to follow! So perhaps it's not the smashing success we hoped would catapult our family into the one percent (I just read in the *Washington Post* that a six-year-old boy made eleven million dollars in one year reviewing toys on YouTube!),[5] but what is priceless to me is walking past their bedroom and hearing peals of giggles as they fumble through their game, recording and broadcasting their work. Our children are privileged to live in a generation where these digital platforms are readily available for them to express themselves. While many lament the deluge of selfies and the narcissistic indulgences of social media, I am grateful that technology has become user-friendly enough that even young children can create their own productions.

Regardless of the medium children use to create, be it YouTube videos, paint, dance, writing, cooking, sewing, acting, or model making, it is crucial to their spiritual meaning-making to cultivate a posture of creativity. And it's the most subversive way to live in a world that dehumanizes us into consumers. Our children are fed a steady diet of media, from books to TV shows to movies to toys that correspond with each program. A large slice of the pie of the billion-dollar entertainment industry is targeting children and youth, expertly designed and packaged to grab their attention. Consuming and creating place a child in different roles, the former being a passive recipient and the latter being an active agent. We need to learn to be both. We need to steep ourselves in other people's creations, learn to appreciate and discern their works, and engage meaningfully within our communities. Becoming culturally savvy is healthy for children as they develop into functional adulthood.

If we remain only passive recipients, however, without generating our own creative activity, our personhood is reduced to the role of consumer, and our agency in the world is whittled away as passivity becomes habitual. In many blatant and subtle ways, corporations targeting children are bombarding them with the message of consumption—that their highest value is in their ability to buy and be entertained. They are robbing our children of their agency to live as creatives by keeping them docile and fed with entertainment. Parenting for our children's imagination means we resist that cultural message. Here is the good news: this is the most fun battle we'll ever fight. Our weapons are toddler dance-offs and kindergarten face painting. Our strategy is as simple as a blank canvas and a paintbrush. Our victory comes not from destruction of the enemy but a finished act of creation: a silly haiku or a selfie with style. Very few of us may raise child prodigies who produce masterpieces, but the battle is won when we have raised children who know they can be a master of their own creation.

This past summer, our family visited a megachurch in Fort Collins, Colorado. As you might expect of a megachurch in an affluent suburb, the building was large with row after row of plush seating. The well-lit stage highlighted a skilled worship band and a charismatic pastor who told funny anecdotes throughout an engaging twenty-minute sermon. The service flowed seamlessly, each detail professionally executed. Like so many in my generation, I am no longer impressed by "churchtainment" and performance. I fingered my smartphone, itching to scroll through my social media feeds. Deciding that it might not fool anyone even if I pretended I was reading my Bible app, I turned my attention to my small neighbors in the pews. Quietly bored, my children had taken to doodling in the church bulletin. In the "sermon notes" section, they had drawn stick figures and speech bubbles with dialogue. I'm not one to save every piece of my children's artwork, so the doodles are long gone, but that moment has stayed in my memory. Sitting in the middle of a worship service (which in many ways, like many worship services, had missed the point), my kids captured the essence of what it means to live. To live is to create, to make beauty in the world that bears one's signature where before it did not exist.

Keeping the Magic

So how can we provide children access to think and express their thoughts? Politicians can invite them up to the front of the Parliament hall. Churches can set up easels in the sanctuary. And as parents we can ask our children, "What do you think? What do you think? What do you think?" We must fight for our children's individuality and creativity in a world organized into systems.

The award-winning short film titled *Alike* captures the bitter reality of the way the systems of our world suck the magic out of our children's imaginations.[6] The computer-animated film begins with a father packing a school bag full of big, heavy books and his child dancing around him in joy. Each morning, the father mindlessly burdens the child with the backpack and takes him to school while he trudges off to his joyless job. At the end of the day, the child jumps back into the father's arms with glee, and his exuberance breathes life back into the father, signaled by turning his father's skin blue. On the way to school, the child passes by a street musician at the park but is dragged away from the performance because school awaits. In school he is reprimanded for doodling on schoolwork and is forced to write his alphabet within the lines. One day, the child jumps into the father's arms but has become incapable of breathing life back into the father—his magic stops working. The next morning the child stretches his arms out behind him, resigned to the crush of the heavy book bag on his shoulders. But the father does not take him to school; instead they go to the park. Sadly, the musician is gone, and the child's face falls. Then the father steps into the place where the musician stood and begins miming music making. The light blinks back on in the father as well as the child, and the magic is rekindled.

No, I'm not anti-school (though I believe the unschooling movement has a lot to teach us), but I want to retain our magic. I don't want to believe it is inevitable that children grow up and lose creativity. We can fight the system. We can bring the magic back by sparking it, validating it, and displaying it on the walls of the Guggenheim.

One of my favorite people in the world is Malala Yousafzai. As a ten-year-old girl, Malala was already a fierce activist for the right to education, garnering national attention in Pakistan. Because of the efficacy of her campaigns, the Taliban felt threatened. Traveling home from school one day, she was shot in the head in an assassination attempt. She was fourteen years old. When she survived, everyone in the world knew about her. Malala has since continued to vigorously use her platform for her cause: the right to education for all.

Malala's widespread influence is due in large part to her own charms and courage. But she has publicly attributed much of who she is to her father, who raised her in a way contrary to the patriarchal expectations of their society. He gave Malala a strong name, after a freedom fighter in Afghanistan. He penned her name into the

Yousafzai family tree, the first woman's name to grace that family tree in three hundred years of recorded history. He admitted her into his school, which in patriarchal societies is a significant recognition of identity and name; it is to declare that this person has potential for a respectable future. As an educator and parent, her father instilled strong values in her by simply appreciating her brilliance, encouraging her to come to meetings with him, and having her and her friends sit with him whenever possible. Indeed, her father, Ziauddin Yousafzai, is a teacher at heart, caring not only for his own daughter but for all the students at his school. He recounts this portion of his life in a Ted Talk, saying, "I used education for emancipation, I taught my girls, I taught my girl students, to unlearn the lesson of obedience. I taught my boy students to unlearn the lesson of so-called pseudo-honor."[7] He humbly insists that Malala is the bold and poised girl that she is today not because of what he did but what he did not do. "I did not clip her wings, and that's all."

Perhaps parenting really is as simple as that.

Dad, there's an eighth of a half of a part of me that doesn't believe in God.

Brendan, age 8

4

HEALTHY
SPIRITUALITY

I know a lot about what not to do when it comes to parenting my kids in the faith department. I didn't want them to be terrified of hell. I didn't want them to view God as the authoritative Bad Guy in the sky, ready to rain down judgment the moment they slip a curse word or forget their homework. I didn't want them to live in fear of the world. This was the way I was raised, and I am still shedding the spiritual baggage of my upbringing, one hefty suitcase at a time.

I was a rather exceptional missionary convert. I didn't just pay lip service but was "on fire for the Lord." I read the Bible, memorized Scripture, prayed, worshiped, and went on short-term mission trips. Eventually I committed myself to full-time, long-term missionary work. My biggest claim to the tribe of evangelicalism lies in receiving an award for my evangelism work from none other than Billy Graham himself. Always an A student, I resolved to gain nothing short of excellence on my spiritual grade book.

Nobody told me this was the one class I could never fail.

As I slowly ventured beyond the small conservative Christian bubble I was raised in and gained a deeper understanding of historical context, I wrestled with how much my faith had been wrapped up in the American culture wars and a certain version of evangelicalism. A long set of discrepancies between what I believed to be faithful to the gospel and what the Christian establishment valued plunged me into a period of brutal deconstruction of my faith. I began to view much of my religious upbringing with a cynical eye. I critically examined the philosophies and theologies that formed my spirituality, while learning to manage my emotional and visceral reactions.

In the midst of a tumultuous faith journey, life did not stop and wait for me to get it together. Shortly after I got married, my maternal instincts kicked into high gear, and before we knew it, we were five years into our missionary vocation, with two kids in tow, and I was on the verge of a gigantic faith meltdown.

How on earth was I going to parent my two children when my own faith system was crumbling from within? What, if any, kind of faith was I going to pass on to them? I desperately wanted my children to have less to unlearn in their faith. I wanted them to have a healthier view of God as One full of endless love and abounding in grace, not the punitive version of God I was taught.

But passing on faith isn't as simple as researching consumer reviews for the best brand of diapers. Faith is complicated and nuanced and laced with our human anxieties.

The reality is that our faith is always embedded in the historical and cultural context of our generation. My job was not to recruit my children to fight my battle against the faith system of my time, but to equip them to build faith resilience in the struggles unique to their generation.

I have fought intense battles in my soul to refine the ideas of who God is and what it means for me to be faithful. And although I am not afraid to share those convictions with my kids, they aren't yet fighting a war. I want to acknowledge and honor the wounds of my spiritual past, but I also want to tend to the spirituality of my children. Living in that tension is what this chapter is about.

Parenting with a Shifting Faith

My kids often bring home ideas about God they have learned from friends or teachers or other influences from outside the home. I worry that in expressing my vehement disagreements with some of these ideas, I am confusing them. How can my children find security in an all-loving God when said God looks different from what Sunday school teacher says and what mom says? But I am learning that we underestimate how much our children are capable of navigating multiple spheres of influence. What if, instead of sheltering them from different opinions and ideas, we expose them to the variety of ways people think about God and faith in the world, expanding their spiritual landscapes? The speed with which information and ideas assault this new generation of young people is unprecedented as videos, images, and clickbait headlines vie for their attention hundreds and thousands of times a day through their devices. They are growing up with a multiplicity of ideas in a way we never did.

Those of us who have faith-shifted, or evolved in our theological convictions, can view the angst of our growing pains as a gift in our parenting. By circumstance, we have had to learn how to navigate different opinions, often-times with people we love dearly. The reality for our children is that they are rubbing shoulders with classmates, neighbors, and online friends from all over the world who hold divergent and polarizing views. As parents, equipping our children with a secure self-identity in a pluralist society has become one of the most important lessons to impart as they come of age. I don't want to beat them over the head with my faith conclusions; I want to offer my convictions to them as a tool in their toolbox so that they can discern for themselves what faithfulness means for them in their own spiritual path.

Parenting with a shifting faith can be confusing and anxiety inducing. But I believe it also places us in a uniquely advantageous position in passing on a faith to our children that is refreshingly authentic. We are determined to show our children a faith that is true, whether our hands are held high on the mountaintops or locked in struggle in the shadows of doubt. We have fought too hard for a faith that is real to settle for anything less for our children.

Just as we talked about extending physical and emotional autonomy to children in the previous two chapters, divesting our power and control over their inherent being also applies to their spirituality. In fact, spiritual wholeness is a sense that our bodies and our minds are fully integrated, and a vibrant spirituality contributes to physical and emotional wellness. Although organized religion is a vehicle through which we can cultivate our children's spirituality, the main difference between toxic religiosity and healthy spirituality is where we locate the child's agency.

Hierarchical religion believes that children need to be converted by presenting them with a set of doctrines and creeds, and that by accepting these tenets they can grow in knowledge and maturity of their faith. Healthy spirituality assumes that children are not spiritual blank slates to be filled with propositions. Instead, children are born spiritual beings; they have an innate spiritual compass that has biological basis. Children who are raised in secular environments still ask essentially spiritual questions. According to Dr. Robert Coles, child psychiatrist and author of *The Spiritual Intelligence of Children*, children actively create meaning out of their natural family environments. In an interview with Krista Tippett, he shares a dialogue he had with a child:

> One boy said to me, "You know, my parents worry a lot." So I said, "Oh?" He said, "Well, they're always worrying about everything." And then he brought up the questions of money and education, but he said, "I think that

they're just worrying that they should really stay around and be with us." So I thought that was interesting. I said, "Is there any reason, do you think, that they're worried about that?" He said, "My father lost his brother." And this just became a poignant story about frailty and loss. "After my father's brother died, my father became more religious," this boy said to me. And then I realized, there he's making that eternal connection between suffering and loss and vulnerability and faith, or the search for faith, or the search for meaning, especially if you've been hurt or you've lost someone.[1]

Psychologist Lisa Miller, in her book *The Spiritual Child*, makes the case that children's spirituality is an indisputable conclusion from scientific research. Spirituality is central in human physiology and psychology, and the evidence is clear that an active and healthy spirituality is linked to children's well-being. However, children in this generation meet with several cultural shifts that present modern challenges to their spiritual autonomy. First is the shift away from religion. Structures for spirituality have eroded as more and more adults, many of them parents, have been raised without a spiritual community. Many parents in this category feel ill-equipped to pass on spirituality to their children, hoping their children will simply discover it for themselves. The problem with this approach is that often children do not find the spirituality within themselves validated and mirrored by the adults in their lives. The second shift is the increasingly competitive climate, manifested in everything from the best developmental strategies and parenting books to overscheduled extracurriculars. In this climate, children are in desperate need of spiritual grounding. The third shift involves widespread fears about global issues. News of global warming, war, political and religious strife, racial tensions, and economic downturn paralyzes both parents and children and freezes any potential for vibrant spirituality.[2]

Knowing that our children are born spiritual and have their own agency in spiritual meaning-making can be liberating for parents who aren't quite sure how to impart spiritual wisdom. We don't need to! If anything, we can learn from them and with them. When my son was nine years old, he asked in the dark stillness before drifting off to sleep, "Why did God invent pain?" Having trained in seminary, I groaned inwardly at the task of translating the doctrine of theodicy to age-appropriate language. I was stuck in the mindset that I had the religious knowledge to fill into my son's empty spiritual bucket. This couldn't have been further from the truth. He had already been exercising his inherent spirituality for his short nine years of life, experiencing pain and struggle, learning language to call the transcendent power he senses as "God," and interrogating the dissonance of benevolence and suffering. He has, from birth, been spiritually active. We explored the question together. I told him about pain that is tangible to him, like stubbing a toe, and how sometimes pain is a warning signal to tell us something is wrong with our bodies and we need to treat it. We also considered whether God is a Being who creates things exactly the way it is in the world. Neither one of us needed absolute answers and we both were satisfied with not arriving at any conclusions. What mattered most was that we voiced our questions and shared our common exploration of these spiritual experiences.

As parents who want to honor our children's spiritual autonomy, we have the responsibility to validate their spiritual experiences and offer them placeholders to express that part of their being. Many people choose organized religion. They take their children to church or synagogue or mosque and participate in rituals and speak the language through which the children manifest their spirituality. Others develop it outside of institutional religion, finding transcendence in nature or family rituals. Miller cites empirical research that suggests that adolescent personal spirituality is statistically unrelated to strict adherence to a religion or creed. The *Journal of the American Academy of Child and Adolescent Psychiatry* published evidence that while personal devotion reduces adolescent substance use and abuse, adherence to religious creed does not.[3]

So what kind of spirituality makes the practical difference in improving children's lives? The research shows that what makes spirituality meaningful is adolescents' personal choice and ownership of their spirituality. In other words, just as it is important for children to know that their body is their body, their spirituality must also come from their own agency.

Belonging over Conversion

Despite the many good things my childhood religion gave me, I feel crippled with spiritual wounds to this day. After years of wrestling with my deconstruction, I believe what brings me the most pain is the lack of consent I had as a minor to agree to an allegiance to Christianity, especially a version that demands one to be "on fire" for God. I appreciate the many beautiful aspects of the Christian tradition, but having been converted as a child with the threat of eternal damnation, I began my Christian life under coercion. My natural spirituality was subsumed by fear.

Extending spiritual autonomy to children means not abusing our adult power over their vulnerabilities by scaring them into conversion. Instead, we can provide spiritual grounding by inviting our children into a large, open field of spirituality where we can play and experiment with a set of values. This belonging allows them freedom to practice their spirituality in a safe and loving environment. Providing a set of values for a child to live into is markedly different in terms of power dynamics than demanding a child adhere to doctrine. The former compels, while the latter coerces.

We named our first child Elizabeth after the character Elizabeth Bennett in Jane Austen's *Pride and Prejudice*. My husband and I love the story of *Pride and Prejudice* and saw in Austen's heroine, Elizabeth Bennett, a strong character who was virtuous and yet was resilient to evolve and grow in her character as her relationships changed her. By naming our daughter Elizabeth, we wanted her to mirror herself after the virtues of her namesake. Of course, she will be different and even more dynamic than this fictional character, but she is invited into the opportunity to become Elizabeth Bennett–like. Our Lizzy will live and create her own stories, but we hope that Lizzy Bennett's story will intersect hers, expanding her imagination of what it means to live a worthy life. Similarly, to give our children spiritual grounding, we offer them a spiritual narrative that intersects with their stories.

As parents, our goal isn't to maintain a hierarchical divine order in the home but to disrupt a world consumed with power, greed, division, and conflict with resistance. We are inviting our children into a family life of developing spiritual habits of power-giving, peace-making, and hope-lifting, that they might radiate these characteristics wherever they move about in the world. Instead of rules to obey, there are stories to create. Instead of demanding blind obedience, we have civil and equal discourse alongside our children about what kind of people we want to be, both adults and children.

Tools of Investigation

Providing belonging as opposed to emphasizing conversion is important because conversion implies a child can de-convert and fall out of the bounds of spirituality. Our faith is a dynamic thing, and our spiritual paths don't follow a straight line. Even at the height of my own decon-struction of faith, I still had periods of earnest belief. Our children will move through similar rhythms according to the ups and downs of life. As they go through tumultuous changes in their bodies and brains, so too their spirituality will be elastic. A strong sense of belonging gives them the ability to flex without breaking, riding the stormy waves of life together with us in the same family boat. Inevitably, our children will experience doubt, and we can help by strengthening their tools of investigation.

Google isn't helpful just when our children ask, "Why is the sky blue?" It can also provide spiritual resources as well. Guidance for using the internet is a subject for another book, but giving our children access to voices that challenge our faith or respond to their genuine questions is important to their spiritual health. By affirming their doubts and questions, we are communicating that their intuition is to be trusted, their emotions are valid, and they have the power to find their own way. Don't be afraid of your children critiquing your personal faith; their irrev-erence will ultimately help them form their own secure faith identity. Encourage them to play with the concept of God. If they get the sense that God is somehow distant and too sacred to make their inquisitions, they may lose their curiosity and miss out on an opportunity to build their spiritual identity. The book *OMG! How Children See God* is a collection of children's words about their percep-tions of God, including having "very big ears" and being of "uncertain gender."[4] Children have vast imagination, and their spirituality can serve as a way of flexing it instead of limiting it via doctrinal standards. Not only does it honor their spiritual agency to imagine for themselves what God is like; they may also challenge our own preconceptions and expand our outdated notions.

If we can think of faith not as something that teaches children propositions but something that tells them a story, it could relieve a lot of our anxieties of "getting it right." No one teaches a story—they tell it, share it, and invite listeners into it. Telling our children our own faith stories is another way to give our children security, not in certainty, but in solidarity. When we share our own doubts, we give our children permission to have theirs. When they see that faith isn't arriving at conclusions, we can invite them to journey alongside us in our faith story.

Freedom of Exploration

I love a segment from the CBS TV series *Young Sheldon* about an intelligent boy who is raised by a very conservative mother. Sheldon goes to Sunday school and argues with the teacher over the logic of his teachings and decides to embark on his own research of people's beliefs. In this particular episode Sheldon's mom sits down next to him at the dinner table, as he is poring over his books, and reminds him that there is only one true God. "That's called monotheism," Sheldon replies and hands his mother a book on the subject. A few seconds later Sheldon looks at his mother and asks, "Would you be angry with me if I don't pick your religion?" His mom, taking a deep breath, replies, "I could never be angry with you. You be a seeker of your own truth."[5] The audience can sense the mother's anxiety over this, but can also see her courage in making space for her son's intellectual exploration.

Vital to the freedom of exploration is the opportunity to become spiritually multilingual. Spiritual multilingualism, says Dr. Lisa Miller, enables children to see the sacred in others.[6] Indeed, the devastating error of my evangelical childhood was the inability to humanize those who worship differently than I do. When our children see others as less than human, it also chips away at their own humanity. I know tolerance of other religions and faiths is seen by some as a watering down of each particular faith—a weak, wishy-washy acceptance of all faiths. Quite the contrary, spiritual multilingualism is gritty work because it requires diligence in learning the tenets of other faiths, the discipline to constantly step outside our comfort zones into unfamiliar traditions, and the emotional resilience to accept critical differences in others because of our shared humanity. These are traits I want to develop in my children to make them citizens of integrity in our diverse world.

Spiritual multilingualism opens up curiosity in children. When children ask questions, inquire of others, and wrestle with the tensions of conflicting beliefs, they strengthen the authenticity and ownership of their faith. As they look outside the bounds of orthodoxy and take risks out of love for others, they grow spiritually. Such exploration serves to protect their spiritual autonomy, because only when they are presented with a wide array of choices and given the freedom to explore can their choice be truly their own. Parents can expose their children to spiritual multilingualism by visiting different religious services—even within Christianity there are diverse worship styles one can explore—reading books about other religions, and, best of all, befriending people of all religions or no religion, cultivating empathy and eyes to see the sacred in others.

The Crucible of Love

Children's inherent spirituality means they have within them the desire and power to love themselves, others, and the world. Granting spiritual autonomy to children means we activate that love engine by pouring in the fuel of our love for them. This requires us to flip the script of managing misbehavior in children by making them feel guilt and shame. Whether fighting over a toy with a sibling or playing a game on the preschool playground with friends, children can sense the tension within them to extend love and generosity or to act in selfish interest. They have a moral compass to rely on; we simply need to call their attention toward it. Honoring their spiritual agency gives them the best chance of living their spiritual potential fully—the capacity to create a field of empowering love, radiating integrity in character that surrounds them and touches the lives of those they encounter.

The response to misbehavior isn't punishment; it is love. When children feel better, they do better. When they are loved, they tap into the depths of their spirituality and access the power to do good. When they act out in hatred and pain, it is because they live in a world filled with strife. Our responsibility isn't to inflict more hatred on children but to work at creating—and inviting them to create with us—a better world where the sacred in me can meet the sacred in you, and together birth more spaces for mutual flourishing.

Hospice chaplain Kerry Egan calls the family the "crucible of love." She reports that at the end of life, what most people talk about isn't religion, or God, or theology, but family. They talk about their moms and dads. They talk about their children. Because our family is where we live out all the big mysteries of life, this crucible of love is where we forge the most significant meaning of our being. "The first, and usually the last, classroom of love is the family," she says.[7] As parents we have a profound influence on the deepest spiritual meaning-maker in our children's lives: a home where love abounds.

To be spiritual is to love, and vice versa. Our children deserve a vibrant, healthy spirituality, and their best chance of achieving that is to be loved unconditionally in the refuge of their home.

The protesters spoke up so people will know this is not fair. . . . It is OK to tell me about scary things because they got hurt, and when you are hurt you have to not keep it a secret because then nobody can help you. . . . We have to not let any more hurting go on—we have to do something about it.

Haydée, age 4

5

PARENTING
FOR RACIAL JUSTICE

I was twelve years old when I first asked Jesus into my heart. But it wasn't until I was thirty-two that I realized I had asked a white Jesus into my heart. Following a white Jesus meant celebrating Christian holidays with presents, candy, and family portraits. Christian hospitality looked like inviting people to a warmly decorated home and serving casseroles and bread, instead of the plentiful seafood banquets in noisy restaurants like we do here on our island of Taiwan. White Jesus would have us worship him in cathedrals that looked nothing like our architecture. Following white Jesus meant that I had to leap across cultures to learn the sensibilities of white culture. As a child, I understood Jesus was white wherever I looked. He was white in picture books, in paintings, and in the movies.

The problem isn't that the gospel is culturally bound. God incarnated into a historical Jewish man and took on distinct cultural traits. It becomes a problem when the group who holds dominant power, financial resources, and global influence is so steeped in its own worldview that

Christians in this group are unaware that their version of the gospel carries elements of culture particular to them.

By the time I went to college, a predominantly white evangelical institution in the suburbs of Chicago, my faith was completely devoid of an awareness of systemic injustices, including racial inequality. Internalizing a way of following Jesus that erased a large part of my own cultural and racial identity meant I was not aware of it myself, and I certainly wasn't able to recognize how it affected others. I distinctly remember a conversation with an Asian American peer in our college cafeteria, in which he was unpacking his distress about being the minority on campus. At the time, I chided him for his anger and negativity, pointing out how our white fellow Christians were nice and loving toward everyone. He looked at me sadly and said, "Cindy, that's just not enough," and walked away. He treated me like I was clueless and didn't get it. And that was because I didn't. The palatable-sounding, universal value of love and equality on our campus had blinded me to the many microaggressions I myself experienced, and caused me to bury the suffering of people of color who have endured it for a lifetime.

In February 2012, a black teenager named Trayvon Martin was on his way home after buying Skittles when he was racially profiled, assaulted, and fatally shot. His murderer was acquitted. And as a free man, several years later, this man auctioned off the notorious gun he used to kill Trayvon Martin. In November 2014, police were notified that a twelve-year-old black child named Tamir Rice was playing with what looked like a toy gun. When the police came, within two seconds of the policemen getting out of the car, Tamir was shot dead. The policeman who killed him also was not indicted.[1]

These incidents of police brutality and racial injustice led to the founding of a movement, including protests, demonstrations, and social media campaigns, all coalescing around the declaration that Black Lives Matter. The statement asserted the humanity and right to dignity for black people in America.

One would imagine Christians could easily get behind this movement, to insist on the right of those made in the image of God to live and flourish in our society. And yet, according to the polling group Barna, only 13 percent of evangelicals, defined as those who align themselves to nine theological points, support the Black Lives Matter movement.[2] Seventy-six percent of evangelicals asserted instead that "all lives matter," and almost the same percentage claimed that reverse racism is a problem in society today. The majority of those polled who denied the existence of systemic racism against black people were white.

Drew Hart, author of *Trouble I've Seen: Changing the Way the Church Views Racism*, says, "Dominant cultures have a way of disguising their own oppressive practices from themselves with strong proclamations of innocence and benevolence and universal principles of equality."[3] This resonates with my own experience of internalizing racism back in college. I knew that I had nothing but love and benevolence toward individual people of color, and

I certainly would have touted the universal principle of equality, but I silenced my Asian friend in that cafeteria conversation and diminished his experience.

The privilege of dominant culture, and of those who have assimilated into it, is to turn a blind eye to the suffering of the oppressed. The cost of dead black boys is far too high for us to ignore the consequences of implicit bias and racism. The conversation on race is painful and complex and sometimes seems hopeless. But as the African American writer James Baldwin says, "Not everything that is faced can be changed, but nothing can be changed until it is faced."[4]

These conversations are critical: to learn the nuances of race, to develop a language for systemic racism, and to understand how to repent, reconcile, and reimagine justice for people of color. This begins in the home and with our children. Addressing his teenage son in his book *Between the World and Me*, African American writer Ta-Nehesi Coates writes, "I would have you be a conscious citizen of this terrible and beautiful world."[5]

Are Children Racists?

A white parent sitting next to me at the playground was talking about the way her children were playing carefree with children of color at the playground. "It's so cute how they don't see color," she said with a soft, sentimental voice. Her apparent belief was that children were able to engage in joyful, imaginative play, disregarding their differences in skin tone. I cringed at the sentimentality and whiteness of the remark. But it raises a question for parents: Can children be racists? Could an innocent toddler with blonde curls and blue eyes and chubby cheeks, trotting around in curiosity and mischief, possibly be accused of being a racist?

The answer depends on the definition of racism. If we define racists to be people who recognize differences in skin tones and color, then actually, yes, studies have shown that even babies as young as six months old will stare at a photograph of faces with different skin tone than their own parents for a longer period of time.[6] The same study follows these kids to three and five years old, asking them to sort decks of cards with pictures of people of various colors and races. The children consistently sorted the cards according to racial lines as opposed to gender lines. Researcher Phyllis Katz, then a professor at the University of Colorado, concluded it simply isn't true that children are color-blind when it comes to race. They are observant and see differences in color. According to some definitions, that makes them racist—though it seems harsh to accuse six-month-old babies of racism simply because they recognize differences in physical attributes between people of different races.

If our definition of racism is malice and ill will against individual people of color, can children be said to exhibit these traits? When I witness a four-year-old shouting racial slurs and taunts on a playground, I attribute his

behavior to what he has heard in his home. Preschool-
ers, grade schoolers, and even high schoolers are rarely
willfully malicious; they are still growing and making mistakes, but we give grace to young people in their errors.
This is why juvenile sentencing is far less severe (although
children of color are disproportionately incarcerated and
given harsher consequences,[7] and some, as in the case of
Trayvon Martin and Tamir Rice, are dealt a death penalty
on the streets).

Children, white children, are for the most part so-
cialized to be civil and respectful of their peers of color,
and yet somehow my black and brown and Asian friends
in college, at the young age of eighteen or nineteen, had
already experienced a lifetime of racial woundedness as
they interacted with white peers. This is because racism is
not and should not be defined as personal prejudice, where
one person overtly hates the other because of their skin
color. In that case, other than a few fringe white suprem-
acy groups, we can basically declare the oppression of racism over in the overwhelming majority of society today.

But it's crucial we frame the conversation using different tools that the field of sociology provides us. According
to critical race theory, racism isn't color-consciousness, nor
is it a personal prejudice against people of color; rather,
it is "a radicalized systemic and structural system that or-
ganizes" the society.[8] When we use the term "systemic
racism," we are referring to the way an entire society is
structured to benefit the dominant cultural group at the
expense of another. Looking beyond individual and per-

sonal interactions, we observe the larger patterns at work in a racialized society. Scientifically, race means nothing. The human genetic makeup originated from sub-Saharan Africa, and our skin color differences have only emerged in the last one hundred thousand years.[9] Yet, as Ta-Nehesi Coates says, "race is the child of racism, not the father." Race was developed as a political and social construct as white men in power developed a racial hierarchy linking physical attributes to designate superiority. In the first decades of European colonization, in order to justify the subordination of Native Americans and Africans, color and biological traits were forged into categories explicitly named as "race." This planted a seed that grew deep roots of racial hierarchy, and this systemic racism flourishes to this day.[10]

Systemic racism is alive and well when white people disproportionately occupy top decision-making positions in both the government and the corporate world. It is at work when the publishing industry is majority white, and when leading roles in Hollywood and television are overwhelmingly given to white people. These are all powerful ways society drives a narrative that centers the white experience, resulting in marginalizing people of color. For example, in 2013 a white actor joked in the comedy *Anchorman 2* that the only sport Filipinos are good at is eating cats and dogs. This movie was released at the height of suffering for the Philippines as the country struggled to recover from Typhoon Haiyan, during which people would rather starve than eat dogs.[11] Racist jokes demean, malign, and erase the history and experiences of people of color in order to serve the purposes of the white lifestyle.

The most insidious aspect of systemic racism is its capability of shielding the dominant cultural group from self-awareness. This is how the founding fathers could own slaves and still draft a document declaring all men to be created equal. It's how the majority of white Christian churches stood against Martin Luther King Jr. in the civil rights movement. By believing our children to be color-blind, white parents ignore the patterns of racial inequity that are entrenched in society and, through their privileged lens, enjoy watching their white children play carefree with black children, while black parents suffer gnawing anxiety as their black boys begin to grow into black men with a system built to marginalize, diminish, and harm them. By limiting the definition of racism to personal prejudice, white parents can go to sleep in peace each night, knowing their children have been taught to be respectful of individuals, while continuing to participate in a society that benefits them at the expense of people of color.

Returning to our question—are children racists?— white children, privileged to be born with white skin into white families, participate in a system that affords them opportunities at the expense of people of color. Scholars argue that children can develop implicit biases against people of different skin color without being explicitly taught to do so. Young children's immature cognitive capabilities predispose them to categorize others in stereotypical fashion and without nuance. Children also pick up social and environmental factors. When their parents live self-segregated lives, where their community, networks, bookshelves, and music collection all consist of a single racial category, children will assume, without ever having been taught, that people of a different skin color are to be avoided or feared.[12]

As parents, we have all marveled at how fast children "soak up" learning, particularly in the first few years of critical learning and development. Because the air we breathe has been systematically constructed to produce a racial hierarchy in which white superiority reigns, kids pick it up remarkably quickly and thoroughly. Social psychologist Mazarin Banaji found that kids as young as three years old exposed to racism tend to embrace it in a matter of days. "We had far over-calculated how long it takes for these traits [evidence of racial grouping according to hierarchy] to become imbedded in a child's brain. . . . This tells us that children 'get it' very, very quickly, and that it doesn't require a mature level of cognition to form negative biases."[13] And those children who are recipients of racist acts and attitudes? They just as quickly internalize their own inferior status in society before they even learn the vocabulary for it.

A Note to Parents of White Children

Before we move on to practical steps in developing a positive and healthy racial identity and providing our children with anti-racism tools, it's important to address how to approach this conversation for both parents of white children and parents of children of color. Research shows that most parents, regardless of color, are reluctant to have conversations about race with their children. Parents of color generally find it more important to talk race with their kids as compared to white parents.[14]

It could seem that for white people, because of their privileges, it's a matter of choice to address anti-racism with their children—after all, white children aren't at risk of being the target of racism. This falsely assumes that racism negatively affects only people of color. The reality is that racism harms everybody. Racism dehumanizes and damages white children by providing them with a skewed social construct and preventing a healthy self-identity within their larger social and cultural environment. When white children implicitly learn from their environment to fear and reject people of different color and then are taught to not express that fear and rejection, they are forced to live hypocritically. They lose the ability to live alongside people of color without anxiety, guilt, and fear. Abraham F. Citron, author of *The World of the White Child in a Segregated Society*, says this: "White-centeredness is not the reality of his world, but he [the white child] is under the illusion that it is. It is thus impossible for him to deal accurately or adequately with the universe of human and social relationships. . . . Children who develop in this way are robbed of opportunities for emotional and intellectual growth, stunted in the basic development of the self, so that they cannot experience or accept humanity."[15]

White children participate in a racially unjust society and therefore experience racial tension and division, and yet, because of color-blind ideology, they have not been raised to talk about these real experiences. White kids know they aren't allowed to be proud to be white, but they aren't sure why. They know racists are always white people and they can't reconcile that with their own skin. White teens often feel uncool because white culture is portrayed as bland and uninteresting. Without a healthy racial identity and equipped with tools of anti-racism, white kids risk missing out on the beautiful richness of meaningful multiracial relationships at best or, at worst, growing into entrenched bitterness, self-hatred, and further perpetrating racist attitudes and acts.

White parents play a critical role in dismantling racism in their own families not only because it is the morally just thing to do but also for the sake of providing white children with a healthy self-identity, one that is capable of navigating social relationships in a complex, multiethnic world.

Let's Talk about Race

"Racism gains power from the silence that surrounds it," writes Sharon Chang in her book *Raising Mixed Race*.[16] She interviewed sixty-eight parents of multiracial children and reports that half of them believed their children were too young to talk about race. Some believed you can't have a complex conversation about race with preliterate children, and others thought bringing attention to race actually corrupts the innocent child. And yet, without intentional anti-racist guidance from parents, children are observing, listening, searching for racial/ethnicity in-groups to belong to, making value judgments along racial lines, and internalizing racism without an outlet to process it or combat it.

Early childhood comprises a child's critical learning years; it's a time when children are making neural connections essential to the rest of their lives. Parents invest vast resources into early childhood, and race, a pervasive influence on one's identity, needs to be a crucial aspect of our parenting.

But first let's just admit it. The number one reason we parents struggle to talk about racism with our children is that we don't even know how to talk about it ourselves. As we have seen, racism is invisible, nuanced, and systematically and intentionally set up to hide its ugliness behind the curtain of faux equality and redirected into multiculturalism. It feels so complicated, so overwhelming, that it's easier to just put off the conversation for another day—or at least until we feel ready. Each day that passes, however, is a missed opportunity for us to engage our children as they internalize the racist structure, and more than likely, if your children are people of color, they are directly targeted by racist acts. My friend Martin says, "What doesn't get talked out risks getting acted out." We cannot wait until we're ready. We can't let the fear of feeling ill-equipped or making mistakes keep us from trying to learn alongside our children as they survive this oppressive system.

I did not do this with my babies, but more and more I see parents teaching their preverbal babies sign language. The reason for this, besides the fact that it is adorable to see their chubby little hands bump against each other with gestures, is that it lessens the frustrations of not being able to communicate their needs, thereby reducing the frequency of tantrums that toddlers are notorious for. It is a powerful tool to be given the gift of language. In the struggle against racism, giving young children a language to process it will empower them by validating their feelings, allow them to address it, and move into a position to combat it.

The insidious nature of racism is a deeply rooted injustice based on racial hierarchy. Simply put, society isn't fair. If you have spent any time in situations involving children + sweets + presents, you'll know that children have a keen sense of fairness. Long before they have words, they feel injustice deep in their bones. From the first time you see your child narrow his eyes and furrow his brow in reaction to his sister getting the larger piece of cake, your child is ready to address racial inequality.

Earlier in the chapter I asked if the four-year-old on the playground shouting racial slurs is racist. And the answer is complex. What we do know is that a four-year-old is at a critical formation period of learning and development. This is a time for his parents and those in community to begin gently correcting his language. Remember, the goal is not to achieve respectability, to awkwardly brush a comment aside and say, "Don't say that. That's not nice." The aim is to teach the child that racist language is based on an unjust racial hierarchy. "We don't say this word because this is what people have said in order to treat people unfairly." Get straight to the heart of the issue, that the injustice of racism harms human bodies in real and oppressive ways.

Young children are also particularly vulnerable to experiences of racism before they have the language to express their hurt. This is an opportunity for parents to be especially vigilant in observing racial attitudes that may be subtly chipping away at their child's identity. It's important to call it out and assure the child that what was done to her wasn't right and that it was not her fault. Help your child engage in the struggle against racism by making what she is invisibly internalizing visible with language. For example, without realizing it, children are reading children's books that are predominantly made up of white characters. In 2014, only 5 percent of published children's books contained black characters. Christopher Myers calls it "the apartheid of children's literature."[17] Our children may not even notice it, but we can call it out, saying, "Isn't it sad that none of the books that we read have characters who are black?" or "You know your buddy Jerome from school? How come none of the picture books have characters that look like him?"[18] Furthermore, some children's books have subtle or blatant racist images and tropes. There has been debate over whether the beloved Cat in the Hat is caricatured as a blackface minstrel. It's important that parents not only stock their home bookshelves with diverse authors and characters but have race-conscious conversations with their kids to help them develop their racial literacy. Organizations like Embrace Race[19] and Teaching for Change[20] offer resources to support parents.

I believe many parents don't engage in these conversations because of a fear of their children becoming pessimistic or hopeless. We want to shelter our children from the darkness of oppressive systems. We want the world to be beautiful and full of light for our children as long as their innocence can be maintained. We must remember, however, that the truest beauty arises out of struggle. By avoiding the struggle and burying our heads in the sand, we are doing our children an injustice—robbing them of the opportunity to struggle against the realities of an unjust society.

At eleven years old, Marley Dias became aware of "the apartheid of children's literature." She told her mother she is "meh" about reading books whose characters are often white boys with dogs. She needed to see herself reflected in the pages of her beloved stories. "I couldn't connect with the characters so I didn't get anything out of the stories," she laments. In November 2015 she initiated a campaign to collect children's books that featured black girls as main characters. She planned to travel and donate the books to other children.[21]

When I read about Marley, I googled her and watched her appearance on the *Ellen Show*.[22] And to my absolute zero surprise and utter delight, she was charismatic, brilliant, well-spoken, confident, joyful, kind . . . and sported big, big hair. So here's what we know about Marley:

1. She is race-conscious and has been from a very young age, noticing how most of the books she was reading featured white main characters. As we have seen, representation of people of color in the media, or the lack thereof, is one of the ways systemic racism rears its ugly head. It erases the identity of people of color, creates a vacuum for positive role models, and inhibits learning and education.

2. Marley understands that it doesn't have to be this way. Racism is not inevitable. Marley was empowered to fight the system with her action. Instead of being a passive recipient of racism, Marley engages with her community to struggle against it. Kenneth Braswell, a father of a six-year-old, wrote a picture book titled *Daddy, There's a Noise Outside* to explain in an age-appropriate way the Baltimore protests going on in the wake of Freddie Gray's death.[23] He says, "Our children deserve to understand the society in which they live. At young ages, they develop a framework of their community based on how their

community impacts them."[24] Developing a healthy racial identity necessarily involves propelling our children into social action. It's a natural response to injustice. Better yet, we can model it by engaging in anti-racism social activism ourselves.

3. Marley loves her blackness. She's not interested in assimilating to white culture by taming her hair; she likes it big and beautiful and wild. Racism does not develop in a vacuum but is embedded in historical, intentional acts that lead to a twisted setup. Tell your children these stories, of how our predecessors inflicted or endured racism, so they find a reason to celebrate their racial heritage. For white children, show them heroes who stood up as allies against racism. For children of color, tell stories of the resilience of their people. Every kid loves a superhero. Show them ones from their own people whose heroism is integrated into their own DNA, and let their pride carry them and those around them to liberation.

George Washington was a he.
And Trump is a he. And Obama's a he, right?
I hope we have a she. It's time for a she.

Clark, age 4

6

PARENTING
FOR GENDER EQUALITY

My grandmother worked hours in the kitchen, expertly whipping up stir-fries over the hot wok. Her face wet from sweat as she chopped and sautéed, she would prepare a table full of hot dishes before her husband came home. Many times, drunk from his business engagements, he'd rage, hit, and flip the table, spilling the contents all over the dining room. My mother grew up in this norm. When my grandfather died, my ah-ma (grandmother) raised my mother and five other children by living off the charity of relatives, doing odd jobs to scrape together bare means. They had a roof over their heads and food for their bellies, though my mother tells me it was a luxury to eat meat once a year during the New Year celebration.

It was assumed that the boys, my uncles, would go to school. Any money for the education of the girls was a waste—girls were to learn housework to be given away in service of their future husbands' families. "They scolded me and said I was disobedient and did not know my place, all because I wanted to go to school," my mother

tells me at the coffee shop, still confounded as she recounts the sharp words seared in her memory after all
these years. "I didn't know that I was doing anything
wrong."

Even though my ah-ma was adamantly against my
mother's education, my mother seems to bear no ill-will
against her. "You know what," she says lightly now, more
to herself than to me, "I believe my mother was very
strong."

Of course she was, I say, and we both smile and pause
to take a sip of our coffee. I admire my mother's resilience in carrying the wounds of patriarchy. In many
ways she is helplessly trapped under the expectations of
her in-laws and society at large even today. Yet I still
delight in our time together as I begin sowing the seeds
of this chapter: how to raise children into gender equality. It is important to me that my mother is with me as
I pen these words, because our work for equality never
develops in a vacuum but draws strength from those who
come before us.

As we sat together that morning, I didn't tell my
mother of my own wounds. Even though against all odds
she achieved post-secondary education, the tenacious
grasp that patriarchy had on her life thrust her forward
into child-rearing. There, it warned through her lips into
my small ears that girls were less capable than boys, that
the top positions of the world were reserved for men. I
must only do the best I can within the confines of this
men's world, I learned.

Like roaring waves, my mother and her mother struggled against the forces of wind and gravity, cresting high
above what was expected in their generation. But waves
crash and pull back sand and gravel, tumbling through
the swirling current before they can push forward again.
Thus is the strength of patriarchy, a system as powerful
and intricate as the oceans of our world. The values den-
igrating women are so integrated into our beliefs about
our worth and identity—indeed, corrupting even our
souls as we yearn for our feminine expressions as image
bearers of God—that we cannot assume progress will
be inevitable, as if power structures crumble merely with
the passing of time and not because of costly revolution.
Only with intentional striving can we continue to usher
in liberation.

We Should All Be Feminists

The first step of intentionality is to name the struggle. I agree with Nigerian novelist Chimamanda Ngozi
Adichie, who says, "We should all be feminists."[1] Despite the loaded baggage that comes with the term,
eliciting stereotypes of women who burn bras, do not
shave, and are militant and aggressive, a feminist is, at
the core, one who believes in the social, political, and
economic equality of the sexes. And for those in the
Christian tradition, we have the additional investment
in the spiritual equality of our shared image of God.

Unless women have the opportunity to live fully into their gendered selves, we are robbed of the complete view of God's image.

Because our liberation is tied up together, patriarchy harms men as well as women. We are so much more than our gender. Our bodies, chromosomal makeup, and hormonal systems are simply the vessel through which we live out our unique selves. Our gender is not our art. Our humanity is our art. Our character is our art. Our stories are our art. Gender is just the tool with which we deliver our art. Patriarchy places twisted prescriptions on both genders, limiting the diversity of our humanity to two minuscule boxes in which men and women must live. Men are told they must be big, strong, and tough to take up as much space as possible to shelter women beneath their shadow. When boys and men cannot achieve these expectations, they nurture their ego to take place of true strength. With that ego, men inflict oppression on women, who are stripped of power by society to resist. Feminism is the movement to add power to women so they no longer need to shrink themselves in order to suffer the indignities of the male ego. When women take up space, men are free to abandon their egos and partner with women for mutual flourishing.

We should all be feminists—fathers, mothers, sons, and daughters. Even though I am far more vocal in my feminism, my quiet husband was the one who painstakingly opened my eyes to the ways I had internalized patriarchy. In the beginning years of our marriage, I fell hard into the traditional roles, which were all I had ever known. I did the grocery shopping and the cooking. When we had babies, I stayed home with them and said thank you when my husband would "babysit" our children. I looked to him to make our family decisions, believing he held the final authority. Exasperated, we would have conversations where he resisted these rigid gender roles I had shackled on myself and, by corollary, on him as well. I'd apologize for doing so and then reflect on the irony that apologizing for my own oppression was yet another trap. Patriarchy was like sinking sand: the more I struggled, the more I drowned.

Slowly through the years of our family life, I was able to tend to my gifts and do the hard work of removing the barriers patriarchy set up in my spirit to keep me from living true to myself. We kept shifting our roles as I relinquished to my husband household chores and child-rearing duties that had never been my strong suit, and laid claims to the things I was gifted at. I am proud to say we are creating a family structure in which our son and daughter see us pursuing our passions that arise out of our personalities, character, and interests instead of our gender.

I began this chapter talking about my grandmother, then my mother, and now my own family life, and that is because our children are shaped so significantly by their first home environment, the only world they know in those tender first years. Beyond the words we use to teach them, they are keenly picking up every social cue as they figure out how and where they fit. But because we carry so many gender expectations from our original families into our emerging ones, it is important we examine what patriarchy has transferred from previous generations in order to break the vicious cycles and subvert those patterns. To raise children into gender equality, we must first and continuously search for the weeds of inequality and uproot as necessary. Living into gender equality is a prerequisite for raising children for it. I will be the first to say it is easier said than done because of how deeply it is ingrained into my spirit. Hopefully, the stake of future generations will provide us the motivation to resist alongside and for them.

For Our Boys

If we only speak of equality as a nebulous, universal value, we will fail to address the very specific ways society sends harmful messaging to dictate masculinity and femininity. To treat an illness, we have to provide antidotes particular to the diagnosis. The diagnosis, we have defined earlier, is the twisted and forced elevation of men over women, which ends up being damaging for both. Keeping the subversion of patriarchy as our end goal, the way we approach teaching gender equality to our children will necessarily be different for our sons and daughters. The corrective they require will be different because they are internalizing a different set of messages. They will play different roles in the same battle for gender equality.

Let's first begin with how to address our sons and the problem of toxic masculinity. Actor (ironically, of the angry monster the Hulk) and activist Mark Ruffalo recently tweeted, "Real men care and real men cry. Real men keep their softness on the surface and their strength inside."[2] What it means to be a strong man, where a man's strength lies, is indicative of a healthy masculine identity. Many in the Judeo-Christian tradition look to Jesus as the ultimate example of manhood. Despite centuries of oppression against women in church history that unfortunately continues to this day, Jesus was an advocate for women. Defying cultural norms of his day, Jesus received and celebrated the ministries of women. He ministered alongside Mary, Joanna, and Susanna. He discipled women and cared for marginalized women, as in Luke's Gospel where he cares for the woman with severe menstrual bleeding. In this way, one can say that Jesus was a feminist and is a grand example of a role model for our sons.

However, the poignant way we can point to Jesus to teach our sons for gender equality isn't through the stories of how Jesus treated women but the way Jesus used power. The patriarchal messaging of the world will communicate to them that they are to gain power and exercise it against others, whether it's bullying with a fist on the schoolyard or manipulation in board meetings or dominion in the bedroom. How can we cultivate a posture of power-giving in our sons that will replace patriarchy with a subversive strength born of sacrifice?

I offer you the answer in the form of our adorable miniature teacup Yorkie. We named her Caramel for her beautiful silky hair in light brown, blended in with strands of black and metallic grey (when her tail wags, it sways her whole body to and fro, her enthusiasm overwhelming all of her two-pound mass). Two years ago, our family welcomed this tiny new member who has seized all our hearts. Now the baby of our family is no longer our son; there is someone even smaller than him, a pet vulnerable to his control. We coached him in how to be gentle with the puppy, warning him that holding her in certain uncomfortable positions can hurt her. At the time, our boy was only seven years old with age-relevant sensibilities despite good intentions. I remember coming home from work to see him holding up the puppy by her front paws and dragging her around the living room. He shouted, "Mom, Mom, is this torturing her? Is it?" as he glided past me with the poor pup and her hind legs helplessly trailing behind him.

Our sweet Caramel survived the two-legged marathon, and it gave us one of many opportunities to speak to our son about empathy, love, and care for the vulnerable. Now, I know a family pet is not for everyone, but with creativity we can find many other everyday opportunities to talk to our boys particularly about how to give away the privileges they will inevitably be accorded because of their male status. One example is how they need to honor consent from women. Dr. Christy Sim, an expert in healing after domestic violence, takes care to talk to her child using popular family movies. She uses the example of Kristoff, the male lead in the Disney movie *Frozen*, and how he asks the princess Anna for consent before kissing her.[3] Our sons are not entitled to touch, kiss, or otherwise make women uncomfortable even if society overwhelmingly makes light of incidents of date rape and other violations. What we can tell our boys is that by giving their power away, they demonstrate true character and strength. A gentle man is one who holds the true power to impact the world for good.

As important as it is to prevent toxic masculinity from infecting our sons, I believe what will ultimately propel the feminist movement forward is to empower women to stop minimizing ourselves and to take up space. By daring to exist fully, we will overcome the patriarchal world. We can do this by showing the boys in our life how to respect the image of God in girls. In 2015 our son watched with us as we fell on to the floor cheering for the amazing hat trick Carli Lloyd pulled off to win the Women's World Cup for the United States. At the time, I hoped and prayed that it would be normal for him to see us celebrating displays of strength and prowess in women athletes and indeed in every field of life. Our desire is for him to grow up into a powerful feminist, advocating for equal rights for every woman. We want to teach him that advocacy for women doesn't mean speaking for them, but making space for them to speak their own stories and life. It is time now to turn to the most critical element of raising children for gender equality: how to give power to our daughters.

Girls and Anger

One of my favorite pictures of myself as a child is of me dressed as a flower girl in a beautiful white, lacey gown. I'm sitting in the back of a car, the summer sun shining through the window, casting a dividing line of light and shadow across the photograph. I was maybe eight or nine years old and I don't remember how I was feeling, but I must have been hot and tired, because I was slouching and sporting the biggest scowl on my face. I love this picture because it reminds me of what would have been erased from my own history—that at some point in my childhood, I was pissed.

As far back as I can remember, I was praised for my smile, my sweet disposition, and my obedience. I don't remember that scowl in the car. What I do remember is forcing myself to smile upon meeting relatives because I knew it would bring me compliments. Most unfortunately, the message to stay sweet and compliant was reinforced by my Christian faith. I was taught that a godly woman isn't fierce but is long-suffering, patient, and gentle. My mother was, and is still, a fierce woman. But I grew up watching the way people feared her strong personality, and the subtle message I absorbed was that anger was not a desired trait in women. Without the opportunity to practice negative emotions like anger, I suppressed the very human parts of myself that contained anger, and in doing so, I shut down part of my humanity and minimized my existence.

We have to let our daughters be angry. Don't joke about girls being full of drama, or shame our teenage daughters for being hormonal. We need them to be angry so they get to practice exerting their existence in a world hell-bent on minimizing them.

Watch carefully when their eyes light up and flash like daggers. Seize those moments, and instead of squashing the negativity, let them speak. Dig deep and ask them why they are angry. Is it because of something we as parents have said or done? This is our opportunity to either apologize or clarify our actions. If their anger leads to destruction, with hurtful words directed at others or us, teach them better words with which to express that anger, instead of shutting down the emotion. Our goal should be to help them manage their emotions as they grow in maturity, not to erase those feelings.

In fact, because our girls will likely internalize a sexist worldview, we need to teach them to be angry. Girls are given the message of absorbing the emotions of others, and compromising their own emotions instead of asserting themselves. Women bear a disproportionate burden of emotional labor. We are implicitly expected to be competent *and* kind in the boardroom, fierce *and* compassionate in politics, and after all that to come home and be in charge of all the details in the home, ranging from birth control in the bedroom to remembering that it's Aunt Stella's birthday next week. We are said to have a natural, biological tendency to be sensitive to the feelings of others, yet studies show those expectations are socially constructed.[4] If we can show our daughters that they can tend to their own emotions, even and especially those that arise because of gender injustice, we can equip them to better live critically into their womanhood. We will need their anger to help make the world better for them and for their daughters, and their daughters' daughters.

"Stay angry, little Meg," Mrs. Whatsit from the novel *A Wrinkle in Time* whispers. "You will need all your anger now."

Disobedience

Ryan Stollar pens a blog post at *Unfundamentalist Parenting* provocatively titled (and in a twist of a familiar religious text) "Children, Disobey Your Parents in the Lord, for This Is Right."[5] Citing Ezekiel 20:18–19, he challenges conservative Christian parenting literature with an overemphasis on obedience. He says, "Just as it is important to teach children to respect authority, it is equally important to empower children to fight against authority." Although the blog was directed toward parenting all children, this concept is especially poignant for girls. We urge children in many religious environments to be obedient, but when boys resist parental commands, we say with a tint of admiration that they are strong-willed, excusing such behaviors with phrases like "boys will be boys." But when girls disobey, they are shamed as being wholly unlikable; instead of just their behavior, their entire personhood is tied up with their lack of compliance.

My husband and I are imperfect parents. We have made overly harsh punishments, misunderstood our children's intentions, and failed over and over again in our parenting decisions. But we can be the first authority figures in our daughter's life that she learns to disobey. It is right and godly and brave for her to buck against our authority when we are wrong—as we often are. Along with apologizing for our mistakes, I want to honor her when she challenges us and stands up for herself. We know the systems of the world are broken, and learning to subvert those systems is an art that requires labor and practice. What better place to start for our daughters than in the home?

Embodied Life

Growing up in conservative Christian culture, I have observed two conflicting teachings. The first is that somehow our physical world does not matter and will eventually be zapped into oblivion—the only worthwhile world is the spiritual kingdom of God. The second is a strong emphasis on maintaining the sexual purity of the female body in order to save ourselves for our future husbands. Abstinence is the only godly way to live. Essentially, a girl is to live as an asexual being until after she has said "I do," at which point she is to serve her husband by making her body available whenever he desires. These teachings are born out of the soil of patriarchy, in which toxic masculinity and sexism are the fruit. Writer Amanda Barbee reports a youth leader who held up a box of donuts at his chest. In order to illustrate to a roomful of middle-school kids the concept of modesty, he leaned over so the donuts were visible and likened it to girls who dress revealing their cleavage. The lesson is that girls' bodies are a temptation to boys' uncontrollable desire.[6]

How dehumanizing to simultaneously be taught that our bodies have no worth in light of "eternity" but, in the meantime, be objectified as a source of sexual pleasure for men. The shame and stigma attached to sexuality are not easily discarded and are brought into marriages, where the mixed messaging continues. There are better ways to teach our daughters about their bodies and remove shame from religious and cultural vocabulary surrounding sexuality.

When my now husband and I began dating in college, we subscribed strictly to purity codes. We were both fairly mature young adults, and despite the toxic conservative teachings we brought to the relationship, we learned to draw healthy boundaries as well as give of ourselves emotionally to build a robust friendship and a blossoming romance. But because of purity teaching, at first we didn't touch each other. What I learned from our relationship is that physical intimacy is an important expression of our emotional intimacy. The magic is not in the "I do" but in the incredibly raw and beautiful dance of risking ourselves in love. There is dysfunction in a relationship when we are vulnerable physically but not emotionally, as in the extreme example of prostitution. But it is also unhealthy when we have become vulnerable emotionally but restrict ourselves physically. Fundamentalism failed my relationship in that I was taught to hold back physical intimacy even when it was good and appropriate expression of our emotional connection.

We have to reclaim the sanctity of our bodies—not as mere temporal vessels for our souls to dwell, but active agents through which we make our impact in this world. In this way, we can help our daughters appreciate their bodies, and not through the lens of magazines that tell them they must be emaciated to be beautiful. Instead, we can teach them to admire their own bodies—regardless

of shape, size, and color—and the diversity of other bodies as an expression of God's creativity. Only through a
diverse representation of body shapes does God want us
to tell our stories. This gives us a foundation on which
to teach our daughters about healthy diet, hygiene, and
exercise. What makes our bodies sacred is not some
twisted purity teaching stripping sexuality from young
girls, but the holy and mysterious embodiment of our
humanity. It is with our bodies that we take up space
in this world—taking risks, making mistakes, learning,
growing, and thriving.

A girl's body does not belong to us as parents nor to
her future partner. It belongs to her. And as much as
possible we can help her practice autonomy and giving
consent to what is done to her body. Long before she is
sexually active, we can respect her body by not spanking
and inflicting pain, by giving her the choice to wear
what makes her comfortable, and by letting her style
her hair the way that most expresses her uniqueness.
In these small ways, she is learning she is in charge of
herself.

We empower our daughters to respect their bodies in
order that they may live embodied lives. The best hope
we have of progress in feminism is if girls learn to take up
space and live out loud. We have yet to see the creative
potential of girls unleashed in society because of the myriad ways women are still minimized. Imagine if our girls
are empowered to live fully into their embodied potential
and beauty in every arena of the world, whether it's in

sports, politics, engineering, business, art, education, or whatever else. A Chinese proverb states that women hold up half the sky. I think if we let our girls shine—they'll light up the whole damn thing.

I work hard to protect the environment and animals near my home. I want my government to work hard to protect my future and the future of the animals and ecosystems in our country.

Levi Draheim, age 8

7

PARENTING
FOR ECONOMIC AND
ENVIRONMENTAL JUSTICE

Having lived in five cities of three different countries in my adult life, I find "home" to be an elusive concept. You may geographically reside in a certain location, but your soul may not yet recognize it as home. That is, until you find a good stylist. Hair people do not just cut your hair exactly the way that makes you happy; they often become good friends, the ones you tell your secrets to.

Two years into where I am living now, I knew I was home when I found my hair lady, Annie. My sister introduced her to me, having randomly discovered her in our neighborhood salon. It was love at first sight. Annie is skilled as a hair stylist but also full of charm and personality. She loves Jesus and cusses a little. Her sharp wit and open sincerity can sometimes appear abrasive. But I did not mind; I enjoyed her refreshing authenticity. We shared our lives as I sat in her chair, where she worked magic on my hair. We exchanged complaints about our husbands. She cheered me on when I started a new business and consoled me when it failed. I followed with delicious delight the tales of shenanigans from her two young children.

Unfortunately, shortly after we met, Annie was fired from her job, likely because her temperament conflicted with her supervisor. I followed her loyally to an independent salon and later when she decided to work out of her home. Finally, as clients fell away and her business became untenable, she and her husband decided to open up a small noodle shop catering to lunch patrons of local businesses. Starting a new restaurant is no small task, but with much diligence and a bit of luck, they were able to get it off the ground.

I sat across from her on a simple stool in her hole-in-the-wall joint and chatted about her new life over a bowl of steaming noodle soup. Cheerful though clearly laden with fatigue, she told me business was going well. We were interrupted by her now school-aged son, who needed help with his math homework. I waited as she helped solve a word problem before returning to our conversation.

"Looking back, I really feel like it was a blessing in disguise that I was fired from my job," she told me. "Although I had steady clients and a paycheck every month, I never saw my children. By the time I came home after long hours, they were in bed. Now, they are with me as soon as they are off from school."

I smiled as I watched her small daughter enthusiastically serve a plate of food to a regular patron the next table over.

As many of us begin families, we too have to negotiate our time, resources, support systems to make the dance of family life and provisions work. Before starting a restaurant and a new chapter in her family's life, Annie faced a demanding job that kept her from what mattered most. Sometimes, steeped in a consumerist society, we fall into the default system and if we aren't aware, we allow it to steal the joy of family life. Consumerism narrates from a single perspective: work, make money, buy stuff, want more stuff, need to make more money, work more, and repeat. Like the frog who dies by slowly steeping in increasingly hot water, we may not even recognize what is killing us. To change the course of events, we first need to understand how consumerism impacts us, our children, and our family life.

A Brief History of Consumerism and Children

Joyce Mercer helpfully locates the story of childhood in the history of consumerism as roughly separated into three periods of the emergence of American capitalism.[1] From early modernism to the turn of the twentieth century, the first period is identified as free-market capitalism. The "free market" removes any interventions, allowing the invisible hand of the market to roam about, shaping it around interests of investors and capital. It is the idea that the forces of the market will somehow settle into an equilibrium that brings about the best interests of the community. Advocates of vulnerable groups contested this, arguing that children need to be protected from the self-interested motives of the market guided by profit. This resulted in legislation to move children from the workplace into schools in order to protect them from the brutalities of the adult world of the free market.

The second period of capitalism, called Fordist-Keynesian economics, reached its pinnacle in the mid-twentieth century.[2] This was the beginnings of a bond being forged between corporate and government interests. The market was to aim for profit, while the government guided society's well-being. Both decided what's best for the world: laborers working extremely hard, getting paid a fair wage, and accumulating stuff made cheaply available through mass production. In the post–World War II era, the good news from this development is that families that were plunged into poverty during the Depression were able to have access to goods inexpensively. The bad news is that it ushered in an era of living centered on consumerism. "Consumption becomes a way to achieve social solidarity—relational connections with others, even as it also marks identity and status."[3]

The home became a place of consumption instead of a unit of production. This was a time when advertising began moving beyond the boundaries of basic marketing to giving expert advice. Mothers were told that the well-being of their children was inextricably linked to a family's consumption choices. Every buying decision became an indicator of good parenting. The sentimentalized picture of the loving family filled with all the right things boosted profit margins of the mass-production market.

Brown stuff begins to hit the fan in the third period of capitalism commonly known as late or global capitalism. Now consumerism has become not just a social cohesive glue but an idol we all powerlessly worship. The machine has been built and depends on continued consumption on a mass scale to keep it running. What do corporations do when people decide they already have all the stuff they need? Convince the public that they need more.

Clothing became more than just something to keep us warm; it became an identity marker, a status symbol, an insatiable chase for the newest and latest. As it pertains to children, marketers developed niche categories of children's games and toys, increasingly segmenting human life into distinguishable age groups, so that five-year-olds can't possibly be playing with "toddler" toys. No, they must buy "preschool" games, only to discard them one year later for "kindergarten" books and toys. Advertisers began to hone their skills of targeting children. Kim John Payne, in *Simplicity Parenting*, cites that children directly impact more than $286 billion of family purchases annually. Advertising spending targeted at children increased from $100 million in 1983 to $16 billion per year in 2009.[4] These numbers are a force to be reckoned with.

Consumerism has a severe impact on children in two ways. First, the thirst for ever more consumption is sucking the souls out of our children. Joyce Mercer says this of her own children's desires to collect toys: "I see how often the excitement and interest in the future purchase hold greater intensity than the purchase of the item itself, which, once obtained, will all too soon be relegated to the bottom of the toy box. The promise of pleasure, however, is so much greater than the pleasure these mass-produced commodities can deliver that it effectively reproduces itself by creating the hope that the next purchase really will be as satisfying as its advertisers claim."[5] Children are taught to be unhappy and discontented, and their hearts become a residence for the entitlement monster who demands to have stuff and to have it today. They are taught falsely that their worth lies in consumption and that products will fulfill their deepest needs. Childhood is now defined as a never-ending quest for fun as boredom becomes recognized as life's most unpardonable sin. A case in point is to trace the trajectory of the birthday party (or any holiday, for that matter). The birthday party has shifted from a simple celebration to what it is today— an enormous cultural pressure to provide exciting games, lavish decorations, thematic cake, hired entertainers, and overflowing bags of favors to send home with small guests. The pressure to be entertained, with stuff, is running both parents and children ragged and dry.

Second, global capitalism and accelerated consumption is affecting the labor market as corporations require more flexible production flows to meet the demands of fickle consumers, stimulating an underground production economy of sweatshops and outsourcing to cheap labor overseas. This creates a less stable employment environment for families, which brings anxiety into children's lives. And low-income, immigrant families often bear the brunt of unjust labor practices. Remember when child advocates tried to protect children from becoming exploited by the brutalities of the free-market economy back at the turn of the twentieth century? Global capitalism has not only impeded that progress but catapulted children back into oppressive conditions. Children today experience less protection than ever because sweatshops slip through the cracks of labor regulation. What is heartbreaking is that much of their oppression remains invisible. When a child of an affluent suburban family buys the latest new toy at Walmart, she is, in her innocent act of delighting in her purchase, participating in the exploitation of unjust labor, often at the expense of another child halfway across the world.

You're Grounded!

Kim John Payne is a trainer and consultant to over two hundred North American schools and has been a private family counselor for over twenty-seven years. He has discovered from years of research and practical experience that the solution to the distress of our youth, which he terms "soul fever," is often simply an enforced time of rest. He tells a story of a fifteen-year-old girl named Margaret, whose mother instituted a quiet weekend in response to a sense that her daughter was undergoing a soul fever. This meant clearing her calendar for a couple of days, to which Margaret responded by exclaiming, "You mean I'm grounded?!"

Decluttering our stuff, our space, and our schedule seems like such a simple solution and yet is stunningly revolutionary in our captivity to global capitalism. Payne reports that simplifying our children's lives increases their well-being. It has the effect of, indeed, "grounding" our children, tethering their sense of identity and self-worth from being tossed about by the dizzying messages of a consumeristic society to the stillness of their souls.

We all are spiritual beings, and children in particular have an immense capacity to connect meaningfully with transcendence—if, that is, we fiercely protect their space (physical, mental, and spiritual) from too much stimuli. Eighteenth-century theologian Jean-Pierre de Caussade describes the spiritual consciousness in children as "the sacrament of the present moment."[6] Those of us with toddlers will resonate with how they have no sense of urgency nor respect for an adult's schedule. If, on the way to the grocery store, they find a fascinating pebble on the sidewalk, they will follow their curiosity with their finger tips. Everything is to be touched, tasted, and experimented with. They possess a deep awareness of their being in relationship with themselves, other people, nature, and God.

Out to the Wild

The 2016 independent film *Captain Fantastic* tells the story of a family whose parents are anarchists disillusioned with capitalism. They choose to raise their six kids in the wilderness, teaching them critical thinking and philosophy and celebrating Noam Chomsky Day instead of Christmas. The parents' strategy against consumerism is to teach their children to climb rocks, navigate by the stars, and eat "real food" sustained by what the earth provides. Although this radical alternative lifestyle of child-rearing may be impractical for some families (and the movie does explore the downsides of living "wild"), the themes of the film tell a truth that resonates: the capitalistic system we've created threatens to steal life from our children.

We live in this world and in systems that contain our lifestyles. It's not possible to completely extricate ourselves from all this, nor should that necessarily be our goal. But our awareness and choices to combat it can shape our children's future. It might be helpful to map out a family schedule and evaluate how much time is allotted to the children for rest and stillness and for being outside in nature, literally grounded in the soil of our earth. I grew up in a big city, but my parents took us out into the country on the weekends. They'd say, "The air out here cleans our lungs from the pollution we normally breathe." Now I believe time spent in the wild cleanses not only our bodies but also our souls. The trees, the mountains, the oceans insist on an alternative story to the one consumerism tells us and our children. Even if trips outside the city aren't feasible for you, there are lots of resources available today on urban gardening, local parks are typically accessible, and the sky is always there for us to look up at. Groups like Green Child and Wilder Child provide ideas for families to disconnect from the frenzy of consumerist society and plug into nature.[7]

The Tree of Sustainable Life

When we declutter our children's lives, decreasing their level of consumption, the end result is not just a child grounded in love and relationships but one whose roots are deeply tethered in order to grow a tree of life and liberation. The metaphor of a tree is particularly poignant as a symbol of a large, looming ecological crisis that directly and deeply impacts our children and their children. Ninety-seven percent of climate scientists, every national academy of science in the world, and the World Bank and the International Energy Agency have all confirmed that we are hurtling toward irreversible damage to our planet.[8]

The results of climate change will be and already are devastating, from loss of lives in Superstorm Sandy to the widespread starvation of the people in the Horn of Africa to the worsening refugee crises. And as always, the first people impacted by this global crisis are the vulnerable, in particular the children. Anthony Lake, executive director of UNICEF, says, "As escalating droughts and flooding degrade food production, children will bear the greatest burden of hunger and malnutrition." He continues with this challenge:

> We have an opportunity to tackle this crisis before it's too late. That means taking decisive action to cut greenhouse gas emissions in order to slow, and ultimately stop, the advance of climate change. It means protecting children whose families are displaced as a result of climate change, and giving children's needs the highest priority in our efforts to mitigate environmental impacts. It means educating children to adapt to the immediate challenges of climate change—and to understand the role that they will be called on to play. Finally, it means listening to the voices of children and young people who, for better or worse, will inherit the planet we share.[9]

And these children's voices are ringing out loud and clear. In 2016, a group of twenty-one youths filed a suit against President Obama, along with federal agencies and the fossil fuel industry, for robbing them of their constitutional rights to live into the future on a sustainable earth.[10] This case, which Bill McKibben has deemed "small children vs. Big Oil," encapsulates the strained tension of our world caught in the toxic ideology of market fundamentalism, where the voices of our children are being drowned out by corporate greed and our failure to act on their behalf. It is also a shining example of children who have taken on the initiative themselves to demand justice.

Kelsey Juliana, the young plaintiff at nineteen years old, had once said, "As a youth, and therefore someone on the frontline of climate change chaos, I have everything to gain from taking action and everything to lose from not."[11] "Sustainable living" isn't just a hipster, tree-hugging, green-liberal slogan. It is pulling our heads out of the sand, recognizing the severity of our ecological crisis, and saying we as collective humanity have made a mess of our world and are making a decision to change.

Ethical Consumption

Becoming ethical, conscious consumers is an effective way to model for our children the values that matter to us. Some families I know are expert thrift-shoppers; hardly any items come into the home brand-new. Their children understand the connection between stuff and the impact that buying choices have on the environment, and their daily use of household items purchased secondhand keeps these issues on the forefront of their minds. In our family, we have started to make the switch to reusable straws, bamboo toothbrushes, and Tupperware for takeout containers. But all the green efforts we make in personal households won't go far unless we also advocate for our cities to support green initiatives. Cities can provide incentives to invest in solar panels, provide quality public transportation, build certified green buildings, and invest in robust recycling programs.[12] As a family, you could support these initiatives and push for further progress as concerned residents. In terms of political advocacy, it's a good idea to follow many indigenous groups who have been water protectors and environmental activists far back in history.

Ethical consumption also means doing research on how items are sourced, whether it harms the environment or children. Child labor is a serious issue particularly in the fashion industry—children slip under the radar in garment factories, spinning mills, and cotton plants. Again, it comes back to telling our children the story of stuff. The things we consume have a trail—a beginning, middle, and end. Sometimes they are made via unjust practices and end up in garbage dumps and harm the earth. The movie turned movement *The Story of Stuff* is chock-full of resources to help our children grow in understanding of their place in the consumption cycle and how best to live according to family values.[13]

The Family Table

The family dinner table is such a focal point of our family lives. In our family, dinner is one of the only times of the day when we gather with our attentions drawn back from the activities of the day. We enjoy the labors of whoever cooked in the kitchen, serving one another by passing plates and napkins and potatoes. Even our dog meanders nearby at dinnertime. (Admittedly, she is largely compelled by her primal food-hunting instincts.) It is a beautiful snapshot of give and take. After all, this is what family life is about—each meal becomes a building block to construct our family relationship.

Globalization, along with trade agreements that provide unfettered access for the agricultural industry to market to the world, is one of the main culprits of climate change. Naomi Klein says, "The global food system now accounts for between 19 and 29 percent of world greenhouse gas emissions."[14] The fact that my family lives in Taiwan but is able to consume cherries from Brazil and beef from the USA is a fairly recent phenomenon. The normalizing of access to global foods is another story of the frog dying in a pot of water heating up—and we have to hop out before the water boils. Our family is making a concerted effort to eat locally produced foods as much as we possibly can. We want our food to have traveled very few miles before making it to our dinner table. This too is an act of grounding our family life in justice for the earth. We want to sustain our bodies with what's been grown in the soil we stand on.

Of course, we are a small family of four, and these attempts feel feeble against the systemic global crisis. What is really needed is to slow down the growth of emissions on a macro level, and we need world leaders to follow through with their commitments to do just that. Indeed, parenting is political, as advocacy for things that impact our society directly affects our children and their future. However, parenting is more than how we vote; it is how we tell the story of our families. Like religious fundamentalism, market fundamentalism wants to hold the script of our family lives firmly in its iron grip.

My hair stylist, Annie, was held captive to the story that dictated she work long hours away from spending time with her children, until circumstances forced her to examine her own priorities. Only when she began living an alternative story did she discover all the small joys of her children.

The reason we flex our imaginations to live alternative lifestyles isn't to express our individuality or to chase the latest trends on Pinterest and popular blogs. It is to remove the scales from our eyes and truly see the realities of what our choices are costing the environment, and then repent and change.

Revolutions require good storytelling. Consuming less and eating locally as a family of four may not drastically alter the rate of emissions, but it is to tell an alternative story with our lives. It is to see the truths of our world and set out on an adventure on the less traveled path—one that leads to justice for the earth, liberation for the children of the world, and wholeness for ourselves. I just know that every epic tale our world has ever known begins with ordinary characters and a motley crew, like Mr. Frodo and his hobbit friends. Our tiny family and eating habits aren't likely to change the world, but they might. And we are on our way to finding out.

We are like little shards of mirror that all together show what God is like. Seven billion shards of mirror.

Ashley, age 11

8

PARENTING
FOR INCLUSION

I had a layover in Los Angeles before flying to Michigan for a biannual writing conference. Pastor Danny Cortez and his wife, Abby, picked me up from LAX, fed me Vietnamese pho on my request for my first meal back in the United States, then took me to their lovely home in La Mirada, blocks away from Biola University. I knew they had four children, but only two of them were in the house when I arrived. Alyssa, a leggy, blossoming teenage girl, and Drew, her youngest older brother, were lounging in their dimly lit living room, having a discussion over Alyssa's new bangs. Upon first meeting, Drew is a bit more shy than Alyssa. I suppose I was surprised by this because Drew's very public story is the reason I had heard about the Cortez family in the first place.

Drew identifies as gay and queer. Every coming out story is significant, especially if, like Drew, you're not only born into a Christian family but your father is a Southern Baptist pastor. Drew's coming out not only reverberated in his own family and his father's congregation but was catapulted into national news when popular blogger John Shore posted the story in a piece titled "Southern Baptist Pastor Accepts Gay Son, Changes His Church."[1] Prior to Drew's coming out, Pastor Danny had indeed had a change of mind from traditional marriage ethics to a gay-affirming one. Pastor Danny's church is now modeling a "third way," an open and inclusive church community that seeks to affirm GLBTQ members and marriages as well as make space for those who disagree.

The response from the denomination was swift. Albert Mohler, president of the Southern Baptist Theological Seminary, penned a scathing article on his website, stating definitively, "There is no third way"—churches, ministers, and Christians must choose to affirm or reject same-sex relationships. And with that pronouncement, Pastor Danny's church was cast out of the Southern Baptist Convention. Before long, the Cortez family suffered the enormous pressure of public scrutiny that naturally comes after the leader of the largest Christian denomination in the nation singles you out as an example of apostasy.

We are still hanging out in the living room. Alyssa and Drew are now showing me how Snapchat works, proudly displaying recent "stories" from their account. Danny had gone back out and brought the kids some Mexican food, which they graciously offered to share with me, as my pho had fully digested by now. Thousands of miles away from my own kids, I was grateful for their company, glad to be welcomed into a family for a few days. For the Cortez family, Drew is queer and Drew is Drew. His queer identity makes him who he is, the son and brother they have grown up knowing and loving. While I was there, Drew received his college acceptance letter from Seattle Pacific University. It turns out Drew had a gay agenda: to pursue his goals and live a life of learning, to love himself and those around him.

I am no stranger to the GLBTQ community. My own family was thrust into the world when in 2009 my trans brother came out identifying as male. None of us, including Aidan himself, knew very much about the trans identity. But with the help of compassionate pastors and counselors, we listened and learned from his courageous storytelling of what it was like to grow up feeling like your biological body did not match who you were inside. The pain of living inside a female body as a man was almost unbearable. He had to dress according to female conventions, check the wrong gender box on forms, go into bathrooms that did not match who he is, and, worst of all, hide and pretend through his formative years—a secret that threatened to destroy him from the inside.

Watching him transition into identifying as male was like seeing a life born again—he is happy, his joy no longer repressed, his body finally one he can embrace. A lot of people ask me regarding his transition, "It must be hard, feeling like you are losing your sister." But I have never felt that loss, because I never had a sister, only a brother who pretended to be one. Having him transition has only been a gain for everyone in his life because he can now be more fully himself. Indeed, Aidan has always been Aidan; his character is the same. Aidan was living life awkwardly, with mismatched tools. Now, with the right tools, he is at ease.

My children have a trans uncle, Alyssa has a gay brother, and chances are you know beautiful GLBTQ people in your own circles as well. As brave warriors have paved the way, more and more GLBTQ people are empowered to come out of the closet, becoming visible in our lives. They are showing us they aren't monsters to be feared but human beings like the rest of us. Progress has come in the way of normalizing the queer community in our midst—they are our family, neighbors, and fellow citizens of the world. It is becoming easier than ever to raise our children without bigotry and hate towards the gay community. It is becoming easier than ever to accept our rainbow kids when they come out, to feel like there is hope in launching them into a kind world that will allow them to be who they are.

Some of my kids' favorite artists, YouTubers, celebrities, and athletes are gay. Ask them and they'll rattle off a long list and tell you what they love about them. They know that Ellen DeGeneres, America's most famous lesbian, loves children and tells everyone to dance and be kind. My kids have friends with two moms or two dads, who love and annoy them just the way their own parents do. The way our children view their GLBTQ friends is markedly different from earlier generations simply because the larger cultural atmosphere has shifted to one of increasingly open acceptance. I often feel like I am the one to be educated by my children and their peers to better understand and love the queer community.

Then Orlando happened. A gay bar, Pulse, was hosting a celebratory Latin night on June 12, 2016, when in one of America's deadliest mass shootings, a gunman took the lives of forty-nine precious members of the GLBTQ community, many of them Hispanic, in their place of refuge. A night of living their ethnic and sexual identity out loud and proud ended in a bloodbath of terror.

When my children saw my distress after hearing the shocking news, I was jolted out of a creeping complacence, a false belief that progress is inevitable without costly revolution. It pained my heart to see their innocence crumble when I had to teach them that, among other factors, homophobia was the reason all those people were shot to death. It is the terrible burden for a parent, that in wanting to learn from my children about love, I must first teach them about hate.

The Church's Complicity in Homophobia

Traditionally, Christian and other religious institutions have held a view of marriage as between one man and one woman, believing GLBTQ individuals' identity to be sinful, one that ought to be repented of. Ministries such as Exodus International were formed to encourage reparative therapy, which includes drastic treatments such as electric shock therapy, to make gay people straight. Pastors preached from pulpits and counseled people in their offices to pray the gay away.

As the wider scientific community continued to research homosexuality, it arrived at the conclusion, in the words of US surgeon general David Satcher in 2001, that "there is no valid evidence showing that sexual orientation can be changed." As a result, popular opinion began to shift regarding same-sex relationships.[2] More and more gay people were bravely coming out. Now young evangelicals are finding friends, family members, and peers who are challenging the paradigms they have heard preached from pulpits, and they are seeing no good fruit in perpetuating a non-affirming theology. In fact, as social scientists have been warning for years, social stigma and harassment of GLBTQ people leads to mental illness, a higher rate of suicide, and a high percentage of homelessness.[3]

In 2013, Alan Chambers, the president of Exodus, shut down operations, publicly apologizing for the pain the organization has caused the queer community. In 2015, gay rights activists scored a big victory in the Supreme Court ruling that same-sex marriages were a fundamental right protected under the Constitution. However, as journalist Deborah Jian Lee reports, having lost the war to legalized gay marriage, conservative evangelicals launched a "Culture War 2.0" by seeking to deny services, housing, and employment to sexual minorities under the name of religious freedom.[4] When forty-nine people were killed in Pulse, just shy of a year from the Supreme Court ruling, prominent Christian leaders publicly shared in the grief of the queer community, and yet some were quite tone-deaf to the ways they may have contributed to homophobia. As Eliel Cruz, bisexual Christian activist and executive director of Faith in America, says, "Christians may not be shooting us. But their theology is leading us to want to kill ourselves. Their theology encourages us to pray to a God to take our queerness away. It leads to deaths in many other ways."[5]

Post Orlando, it is more important than ever for those in faith communities and other communities to raise our children into an affirming stance that celebrates queer identity and allows GLBTQ people full inclusion into marriage, membership in church and other faith communities, and equal opportunities in every arena of society.

Gender and Sexuality 101

The issue of sexuality has become a contentious battleground for the latest culture war. Culture wars are fanned by propaganda, appealing to the populace's basest emotions of fear and hate. To combat homophobia, we can overcome the ignorance of propaganda with a curiosity for scientific understanding of our gender and sexuality. As parents who have birthed complex human beings into this world, we have the responsibility to understand as much as possible the biological formation of who our children are as we nurture them during their formational years.

When I was pregnant with my babies, especially with my firstborn, I pored over pregnancy magazines and books, subscribing to BabyCenter ticker trackers, which sent me updates on the development of my baby at fourteen weeks, nineteen weeks, and weekly in the third trimester. I watched with wonder at the computer graphics of how the alien-looking blob formed little hands and feet, and watched with relief as the oversized head eventually grew into proportion with the rest of the body. But in all the pregnancy books I read, it was always assumed my child would be a boy or a girl. Of course, publishers of such books need to cater to mass appeal, meeting the needs of the majority of parents whose babies fall into gender binaries. They also don't want to bore non-medically inclined readers with the nuances of our sexual makeup. But, as it turns out, those details are important, and knowledge of gender and sexuality can become life-saving in contrast to deadly homophobia.

Pediatrician Joani Lea Jack lays out a simple but thorough timeline of gender and sexual development from the womb in her excellent blog post "Unfolding Miracles: Human Sexuality."[6] She takes us from the beginning of our journey of life with our set of twenty-three pairs of chromosomes, one of which is the sex pair. It contains the blueprint for the development of our internal sex organs. These are the sex organs that aren't visible from the outside but are vital in dictating the next phase of development: sex hormones. Among internal sex organs, ovaries mostly secrete estrogen, while testes mostly distribute testosterone. Sex hormones dictate the formation of external sex parts, either a penis or a vagina. And by the end of the first trimester, most of the time it is clear whether the baby will be a boy or girl according to the baby's external sex organ.

For the most part, this is what we know of gender. From whatever external sex organ the obstetrician visibly observes from the ultrasounds toward the end of the first trimester, it is declared whether we are having a son or daughter. But actually there's more.

After the formation of external genitalia, the sex hormones' jobs aren't yet done. They still have to develop our brain sexuality, which takes place in the second and third trimesters. Brain sexuality is the brain science of why and how we exhibit certain traits that correspond to our gender and sexuality. The way our brains are structured is impacted by the way the sex chromosomes, the internal sex organs, and the hormones they secrete interact intricately with one another. Already we are gaining a depth of complexity of our sexuality from following this pathway. The line traced from our sex chromosomes, to internal sex organs, to hormones, to external sex organs, to brain sexuality isn't straight and narrow but branches into millions of diversions that make each individual baby so fantastically unique it is mind blowing.

It wasn't until my brother Aidan came out as trans that we learned there are babies who are intersex, exhibiting "ambiguous genitalia," carrying traits of both male and female internal/external organs. And here, we haven't even gotten into gender identification and sexual orientation yet.

According to Dr. Joani, gender identity, although determined by the second or third trimester, isn't expressed until children are eighteen months to three years old. If you ask a three-year-old, "Are you a boy or a girl?" sometimes the answer matches their external genitalia and sometimes it doesn't. As we are learning, gender identity is affected not only by external genitalia but also by sex chromosomes, internal genitalia, hormones, and brain sexuality. We cannot see the wind blow, but it doesn't mean air currents don't exist. What lies invisible to us is still powerfully at work in our gender identity. Lastly, our sexual orientation, the gender to which we are attracted, is also woven together wonderfully in our mother's womb (second or third trimester) but, like gender identity, isn't expressed until outside the womb, typically around the time of puberty.

I live in a bustling city full of glamorous lights that stay on deep into the night. Recently, my family and I took a two-hour trip out to the beach. In the quiet of the evening, my daughter and I decided to take a stroll. After a while, we stopped and stood on the ocean-soaked sand with waves gently lapping our toes and stared up into the dark expanse where numerous stars sparkled. The longer we stared, the more stars became visible. It doesn't take long to become utterly humbled when considering how minuscule we humans are in light of the vast universe. As we have learned more about the universe, we have had to shift our preconceived notions and readjust our worldview accordingly. Discovery leads to paradigm changes. We can choose to let these changes suffocate us into panicked breathlessness, or we can breathe deeply of the majesty and mystery of the unknown. We can choose to reject the god of the gaps (a term that refers to relegating whatever is scientifically unexplainable to the work of God), or we can let scientific discovery lead us into deeper reverence of the way God has worked beyond our imagination.

In her blog post, Dr. Joani chooses the latter. The complexities of our biological systems that determine our gender and sexuality will yield new understandings of why people identify as GLBTQ. We can retreat into panic of the unknown and add to the injuries that the church has inflicted on the queer community, or we can let the queer community lead us into deeper understanding of who God is and how God has created them queer and beautiful and beyond what we had ever imagined about what it means to be human.

I didn't talk to my daughter that night about the stars, about how many light-years each of them traveled before their sparkles became visible to our naked eye. I just let her soak in the beauty of the sky. I want her spirit to be moved before learning the head knowledge. In the same way, even as I learn more about the biology of GLBTQ persons, I most likely won't explain these details to my kids but simply let them enjoy the marvel of GLBTQ people in their lives. Regardless of whether you want to raise your children as pro-GLBTQ or have a child who identifies as GLBTQ, learning to celebrate the queer community will benefit us all.

Uniquely You

Many queer kids report knowing they are somehow different from a very young age. Think of the kid who was assigned the male gender at birth but who enjoys dressing up as a princess or growing long hair, or the teenager who realizes she likes girls while the other girls have crushes on guys. While it has taken me years of life experience to slowly learn to be myself, many young queer people have been forced to learn this lesson earlier in life. By the time they have found a safe space to express themselves, they are comfortable in their skin in a way many others aren't.

As parents, we can amplify the courage in GLBTQ youth and celebrate unique expressions of self. In this way, our children know they are safe to be who they are. Regardless of our children's gender identity and sexual orientation, we all have closets in which fear keeps our gifts at bay. Creating room for marginalized youth such as GLBTQ makes it possible for them to survive as well as expand space for all youth for more love, inclusion, and diversity of expression.

Activism

We tend to think of activists as people who are natural-born charismatic leaders—loud, outgoing, forceful people who demand change. This may be true of some, but many of my GLBTQ friends exhibit personalities of all stripes. Some are timid and others are conflict averse, and yet from the vantage point of a marginalized existence, they know activism is a necessity for them and for those in their own community. They do the hard work of developing their own voices and find their platforms to insist on change for a better world. The historical progress and advancement toward GLBTQ equality is the fruit of generations of effective activism. For example, within six days of the Orlando massacre, GLBTQ advocates quickly mobilized to form a group called Gays Against Guns, protesting on Fifth Avenue in New York City, channeling their grief into activism against gun violence.[7]

If as parents we want to raise our children in a faith tradition that centers on the building of justice, righteousness, and mercy in the political world we reside in, there's no better role model to look to than the queer community. Faithfulness translates into social action. Speaking of faithfulness, the queer community is also a people leading the way on spirituality.

Faithfulness

Nothing ramps up my cynicism more than the infuriating homophobia inflicted by Christian institutions. In Taiwan, considered one of the most GLBTQ-friendly nations in Asia, the loudest voices that mobilize against civil liberties of the queer community are Christian groups. The culture war against GLBTQ has been exported even to my corner of the world. This hateful agenda threatens to drive a wedge between those who identify as queer and also identify as Christian. The truth is, GLBTQ people are sitting in the pews of churches, leading Bible studies, and playing drums on the worship team. There is no dichotomy between being gay and being Christian, despite the rhetoric propagated by mainstream evangelical media.

A 2015 Pew Research Center survey showed that as Christianity has declined overall in America, 48 percent of GLBTQ Americans identify as Christians—a 6 percent increase from 2013. How can it be, that in facing some of the worst vitriol from the Christian church, GLBTQ people are running toward this faith? My friend, blogger Ben Moberg, who is himself gay, says it best: "God dwells in the margins. Walter Brueggemann once said, 'the arc of the gospel is bent toward inclusivity.' And you only need to read the same book that has been shot like a dagger at the queer community to see that this has been the liberating story all along. God always drops anchor with the exiles. God lifts up the voices of the outcast in defiance of those that would say God's love only goes so far, that God's image is only reflected in a favored few."[8]

If anything, queer people of faith can be instrumental in helping faith communities explore deeper, more nuanced expressions of spirituality because of the ways they embody an intersection of identities and break down hierarchies propped up by systems of power. Queer kids, teens, and adults coming out of the closet disrupt the ways traditional faith has been practiced, specifically through a white, cis-heteronormative lens. In order to acknowledge the diversity along the gender-identity and -orientation spectrum, we are compelled to consider the ways we have erased and missed the mark in our theologies. As queer Christians engage in meaning-making within faith communities more openly, we all benefit from a healthier expression of spirituality, one that liberates all of us from limiting identities. Although I am cisgender and straight, queer Christians stretching boundaries make space for me to practice my femininity beyond the borders of what white patriarchy has restricted in my gender expression. This allows me to be more authentic in my connection with God and others.

Certainly, this is what I want for my own children. I don't want their view of God to be mediated by a white, cis-hetero, patriarchal lens, and I want them to playfully engage with their developing identities. I desperately need our faith and spirituality to be rainbow colored, shaped and shaded by queer people of faith, in order to expand our notions of what it means to be faithfully human.

Adults like us when we have strong test scores,
but they hate us when we have strong opinions.

Emma Gonzales, age 18

9

CHILDREN AS RADICAL HOPE

In 1963, Martin Luther King Jr. delivered an iconic speech at the Lincoln Memorial. The speech became titled for its rousing refrain "I have a dream." And at the epitome of that section, the climax within the climax, King delivers what he knows will drive people to action: "I have a dream that my four little children will one day live in a nation where they will not be judged by the color of their skin but by the content of their character."

Fifty-five years later, in the wake of Martin Luther King Jr.'s legacy, another central figure arose in the unlikely space of the entertainment industry, Oprah Winfrey. While receiving Golden Globes' annual Cecil B. DeMille award for lifetime achievement, the popular talk show host and activist chose to use her platform to highlight the growing #MeToo movement, to believe women when they report sexual harassment/assault and to hold men accountable. She told the stories of Recy Taylor, a black woman raped and denied justice in the Jim Crow era, and Rosa Parks, a black woman who refused to give up her bus seat in segregated America. Then she got a little louder in her speech, just as King increased his volume when telling us his dreams, and she said, "So I want all the girls watching here, now, to know that a new day is on the horizon." Those of us who heard the speech live will remember the chills that ran down our spines as that beautiful vision of justice beamed into that awards ceremony via Oprah's booming voice and was broadcast into our spirits all around the world.

What these powerful figures knew, in their fight for their respective movements of their time, is that children are our radical hope.

I remember one Christmas when we gathered with four generations of family, and as is often the case when a family is populated with young children, all we did was sit around and enjoy toddler antics with bright smiles on our faces and joy in our hearts. Great-grandma commented, "Children are such a blessing," much like the cross-stitch sayings embroidered on the pillows on her couch. As much as I agree with the sentiment (how can you disagree with a grandma's love?), I feel as though it doesn't come close to capturing the depth to which children bring us healing and wholeness. Blessing connotes an aftereffect, a benediction tacked on at the end, a cherry on top of the real dessert. My hope is that this book has served to persuade you that children are so much more than cute little humans-in-the-making here to give us delight during their season of smallness, indeed that they are fully human beings who need to be integrated into the central fabric of our society. They do bless us with their adorable beings, but they also change us, change the world, and inject a vitalizing hope into sustaining our humanity from generation to generation.

Changing Us

When I was little, I remember my siblings getting sick and vomiting and watching my mom clean up their mess, thinking, *I could never do that. Gross!* Today, I clean up vomit and watch the same thought cross my children's minds. Somehow, between being a child and becoming a parent myself, I figured out how to overcome a gag reflex and deal with upchuck. We become capable of doing things we never thought possible because parenting introduces responsibilities that demand what the young people say these days, "adulting."

Just the other day, my son got hurt with a deep gash to his side, requiring a trip to the emergency room and follow-up wound dressing. Having always been squeamish around blood, I rose to the occasion and looked square at the gaping wound in order to help him dress it at home. Of course, parenting doesn't just help us overcome the gross factor, but children draw out courage and resilience in us that we never knew existed. In healthy parenting, they make us become better versions of ourselves. The phrase "mama bear" refers to the maternal instinct to protect our children from anyone seeking to harm them, so we learn to develop an armor and a fierce ferocity that we perhaps never had for ourselves. And yet, after having children, especially in the early days aided by hormones, it is difficult to watch the news or read about human suffering in any form without the thought crossing our minds that this suffering human is someone's baby, and we become reduced to useless puddles of grief and sorrow. Children make us stronger and softer than ever. They compel us to be larger versions of ourselves—higher, deeper, fuller versions of being human.

Children take us back to our own childhood, for better or worse. They afford us opportunities to revisit the beautiful nostalgia of our past, recreating our favorite childhood traditions, getting down on the floor to play with the same childhood toys, and serving them our favorite childhood snacks. One of mine is a beverage popular in Taiwan called Marble Soda. It's served in the 1980s Coke-style glass bottle but with a twist. At the neck of the bottle, there's a special design that keeps a marble lodged within it. When you swig the soda, the drink passes through the marble making it spin. When I eagerly bought my kids one just to relive my own nostalgia, my husband noted how much of a choking hazard it was, which is a very fair point. They tried it once and we'll stay away from marble sodas from now on, but it felt important for my kids to experience my childhood beverage, at least once, with careful supervision.

On the flip side of reliving childhood joy is dredging up childhood pain. I've mentioned earlier in the book that verbal scolding was a part of my childhood and something I did not want my children to receive. And yet I often found myself repeating those patterns in my own parenting, because my children's behavior triggered the scolding I received, and my first instinct is to fall into the cycle of shame. Here's why: because I am still in pain. I have yet to face the shame I internalized, so it has stayed on the surface of my interactions with my children, making it my instinctual response. In order to do better by my kids, I am motivated to look deeply into my own baggage and unpack it instead of handing it down to them. When I have sufficiently dealt with the pain of my own shame, the response I have for my children will not be more shame, but gentleness—for the child in me, and the child before me. Not every parent does this work, but brave cycle-breakers do. When asked how we can connect better to our children, Dr. Shefali Tsabary, clinical psychologist and author, says, "You should first connect to yourself. The extent to which you, yourself are a deeply grounded being, detached from the vagrancies of life, that is the extent in which you will be able to usher your children."[1] This goes beyond the "oxygen mask" analogy, that in order to take care of your children you must take care of yourself. It is that our children fundamentally take us into a nosedive into the levels of ourselves that require dismantling and rebirth—they are raising us as much as we are raising them.

Changing the World

"I want to change the world, with words," says storyteller and poet Joel L. Daniels, author of *A Book About Things I Will Tell My Daughter*.[2] When you love someone, your love spills over to art and activism, a fierce determination to change the world because it can never be good enough to be worthy of the presence of your child. In America's recent history, it would be hard to find a chapter darker than the tragedy of the Sandy Hook shooting, when a terrorist gunned down twenty kindergarteners at Sandy Hook Elementary School in Newtown, Connecticut, on December 14, 2012. Shannon Watts, a mother who was folding laundry at home when the news broke, began a grassroots movement that flourished into the organization Moms Demand Action for Gun Sense in America.[3] It doesn't have to take a mother's heart to know something ought to change in a nation where children are murdered in cold blood, but this particular mother's heart propelled her into action.

In 2016, alongside drag queens and gay activists marched a Chinese grandma in her late sixties for the fight for marriage equality in Taiwan. I stood next to her and watched her wave wildly and give the thumbs up signs to men in skimpy underwear on floats, who were more than delighted to respond enthusiastically with cheers. That woman is my mother. She isn't an activist or a politician, but she has a trans son. She marched for a better world because she knows other families like ours deserve equality. Six months later, the Constitutional Court of our country ruled in favor of same-sex marriage.

Because of the children, we make art, we march, and we scrap the current vision of reality in exchange for one that makes space for our children to flourish. Our children are unique beings, and when they make an entrance into our world, they both change the world and demand that the world change for them. So often we are pressured by society to mold our children to fit the world, when what is more true is that the world isn't ready enough to contain their spirits. We discover this when we get up close in listening and getting to know our children, when we make ourselves willing to be astonished by their particular blend of personality and spark. When that happens, the realization dawns: Oh no, we cannot tame the spirit out of this child; we have to quiet the world enough to hear her sing. Not because we want to silence others, but because we know that when the audience chatter dies and her voice rings out, we all will benefit from her art. Our children compel us to stretch the world into greater beauty, into a place where everyone gets a chance on the platform and the rest of us get the chance to applaud in jubilee. We make the world more kind, more just, more generous because we know our children deserve it.

An eight-year-old black boy named King Johnson wrote the following in a journal entry for school on January 22, 2018:

Today was not a good learning day. blah blah blah i only wanted to hear you not talking. You said something wrong and i can't listen when i hear lies. My mom said That the only christofer we actnokledg is Wallace. Because Columbus didn't find our country, the Indians did. I like to have columbus day off but I want you to not teach me lies. That is all. My Question for the day is how can white people teach black history? King Johnson

The teacher commented she was disappointed in this journal entry. But the internet was not. The post went viral as people celebrated not just the kid's spunk but also the mother for raising him right.[4] In a short journal entry, King Johnson managed to burn both a white supremacist history and the education system that delivers it, and he did it by referencing pop culture (Christopher Wallace is the American rapper better known as B.I.G.), with a lot of sass, while retaining his childish desires to have school off. It is hard to imagine a better way to confront heavy social justice issues than with the wit and authenticity of an eight-year-old boy.

In 2018, a school mass shooting occurred in Parkland, Florida, taking the lives of fourteen students and three staff members. It was a horrific tragedy, yet a familiar despair set in because everyone knows that the death of twenty kindergarteners in Sandy Hook in 2012 hadn't been enough to propel changes in gun-reform policy. Why would this be any different? But it was different, because this time the friends of the victims were fierce teenagers. Teenagers who had been educated in a well-resourced school like Parkland, trained in debate, and sharpened with critical-thinking skills. Teenagers who were well versed in platforms like Twitter, where they dragged adult politicians with ease, subverting the power structure. Those who had nothing to lose (students demanding their own safety) went head-to-head with lawmakers who had everything to lose (those who accept large donations from organizations like the National Rifle Association).[5] A small group of grieving teenagers, shaken from violent trauma in their community, managed to amass a major social movement in hopes that #NeverAgain will there be a mass shooting in schools. It is one of the most hopeful things I've ever witnessed—children saving themselves.

Jason Reynolds, a best-selling young adult novelist, told *The Daily Show*'s Trevor Noah that he spends time with young people, his target audience, because they are "the key to hopelessness."[6] He shows up to tell them, "I am you and you are me, I've been where you are, and you're going hopefully far beyond where I will ever go." These simple words capture the spirit of how children inject a vitalizing hope and purpose to our being in the world, while not reducing them to objects of inspiration. The children propel us into fighting for a better future because we belong to one another. We can see ourselves in our reflections of each other—our childhood in them, their future in us.

The social justice landscape in which activists and writers like myself operate can quickly become exhausting. From the scale of the problems we confront, to the infighting of our various movements, to the rapid pace of changes—learning to sustain ourselves for the long haul is the key to making progress. And the main ingredient for sustainability is none other than hope.

Sometimes we are so focused on the potential of children to grow into whatever exciting persons they may be that we forget that they already are those persons, and that their potential may not be lying in the future but embedded within them in the present. Our hope for the world isn't just in waiting for the next generation to rise up for change; it is mining for the hope they generously gift us, if only we have the eyes to see and the ears to hear. It is never a waste of time or energy to sit in the presence of a child. It is through time with them that we access the wellspring of joy for our flourishing both now and in the future. Let us give to our children so that they might give back, and may the cycle of lovingkindness unfold our world into a more peaceful and just place.

For our children and our children's children.

Notes

1. Antonio Franco Garcia, "7 Facts about Child Poverty You Should Know," *UNICEF Connect*, October 15, 2015, https://blogs .unicef.org/blog/7-facts-about-child-poverty-you-should-know/.

2. Naomi Klein, "Climate Change Is Intergenerational Theft. That's Why My Son Is Part of This Story," *The Guardian*, November 6, 2016, https://www.theguardian.com/environment/2016/ nov/07/climate-change-is-intergenerational-theft-thats-why-my-son-is-part-of-this-story.

3. Annie Kelly, "Money 'Wasted' on Water Projects in Africa," *Katine Chronicles Blog, The Guardian*, March 26, 2009, https://www .theguardian.com/society/katineblog/2009/mar/26/water-projects -wasted-money.

4. Health Encyclopedia, University of Rochester Medical Center, s.v. "Understanding the Teen Brain," https://www.urmc .rochester.edu/encyclopedia/content.aspx?ContentTypeID=1& ContentID=3051.

5. "About Adverse Childhood Experiences," Centers for Disease Control and Prevention, https://www.cdc.gov/violencepreven tion/acestudy/about_ace.html.

6. Neta C. Crawford, "US Budgetary Costs of Wars through 2016: $4.79 Trillion and Counting" (paper, Watson Institute of International and Public Affairs, Brown University, September 2016), https://www.brown.edu/web/documents/nosearch/2016Costsof War.pdf.

7. Hanna Rosin, "How a Danish Town Helped Young Muslims Turn Away from ISIS," *Health News from NPR*, July 15, 2016, https://www.npr.org/sections/health-shots/2016/07/15/485900076/ how-a-danish-town-helped-young-muslims-turn-away-from-isis.

8. Annie Reneau, "A Love Letter to the Cycle Breakers," *Motherhood and More* (blog), http://www.motherhoodandmore .com/2015/12/a-love-letter-to-the-cycle-breakers.html.

9. Elyse Wanshel, "This #WokeBaby Made Her Own Adorable Sign for the Women's March," *Huffington Post*, January 23, 2017, https://www.huffingtonpost.com/entry/toddler-protest-sign-wom ens-march-washington-charlotte_us_5886ifcce4b096b4a2330682.

10. "Youth in the Civil Rights Movement," Civil Rights History Project, Library of Congress, https://www.loc.gov/collections /civil-rights-history-project/articles-and-essays/youth-in-the-civil -rights-movement/.

11. Cindy Brandt, "The Gospel according to Moana," *Unfundamentalist Parenting* (blog), April 19, 2017, http://www.patheos .com/blogs/unfundamentalistparenting/2017/04/gospel-according -moana/.

12. Mark Mancina, Opetaia Foa'i, Lin-Manuel Miranda, "I Am Moana," in *Moana (Original Motion Picture Soundtrack)*, Walt Disney Records, 2016.

13. Mark Mancina, Opetaia Foa'i, Lin-Manuel Miranda, "Know Who You Are," in *Moana (Original Motion Picture Soundtrack)*, Walt Disney Records, 2016.

CHAPTER 1

1. Robin Grille, *Parenting for a Peaceful World* (Avalon Beach, Australia: Vox Cordis Press, 2013), 19.

2. Grille, *Parenting for a Peaceful World*, 21.

3. Grille, *Parenting for a Peaceful World*, 72.

4. William Sears and Martha Sears, *The Fussy Baby Book* (New York: Little, Brown, 1996).

CHAPTER 2

1. https://youtu.be/uGtLWQsQ8HU.

2. Ksenia Bystrova et al., "Early Contact versus Separation: Effects on Mother-Infant Interaction One Year Later," *Birth* 36, no. 2 (June 2009): 97–109.

3. Carolyne Willow and Tina Hyder, *It Hurts You Inside: Children Talking about Smacking* (London: National Children's Bureau, 1998), 26–27.

4. Amy McCready, "Spanking from a Child's Perspective," Positive Parenting Solutions, https://www.positiveparentingsolutions.com/parenting/spanking-from-childs-perspective.

5. See Elizabeth T. Gershoff and Andrew Grogan-Kaylor, "Spanking and Child Outcomes: Old Controversies and New Meta-Analyses," *Journal of Family Psychology* 30, no. 4 (June 2016): 453–69.

6. See Brendan L. Smith, "The Case against Spanking," *Monitor on Psychology* 43, no. 4 (April 2012): 60, http://www.apa.org/monitor/2012/04/spanking.aspx.

7. Peter Swindon, "Revealed: Pro-smacking Lobbyists Funded by Christian Fundamentalists," HeraldScotland.com, October 29, 2017, http://www.heraldscotland.com/news/15626142.Revealed__Scotland__39_s_pro_smacking_lobby_funded_by_Christian_fundamentalists/.

8. Josiah Hesse, "Billy Graham's Grandson Says Protestants Abuse Kids Just Like Catholics," Vice.com, August 25, 2017, https:// www.vice.com/en_us/article/xwwd3w/billy-grahams-grandson -says-protestants-abuse-kids-just-like-catholics.

9. "Paradox #3: Freedom Leads to Self-Control," *Untigering* (blog), November 27, 2017, https://untigering.com/paradox-3-free dom-leads-to-self-control/.

10. Bromleigh McCleneghan, *Good Christian Sex: Why Chastity Isn't the Only Option—and Other Things the Bible Says about Sex* (San Francisco: HarperOne, 2016), 69.

11. Toby Morris, "The Pencilsword: No 'I' in Sex," The Wireless, March 24, 2017, http://thewireless.co.nz/articles/the-pencilsword -no-i-in-sex.

CHAPTER 3

1. "Watch: Jacinda Ardern Interrupts Speech to Warmly Welcome Delighted School Kids into Room," TVNZ, December 5, 2017, https://www.tvnz.co.nz/one-news/new-zealand/watch-ja cinda-ardern-interrupts-speech-warmly-welcome-delighted-school -kids-into-room.

2. "Smuggling Hope," https://www.youtube.com/watch?v=ZlX otE8Pg4Y.

3. Colleen Gillard, "Why the British Tell Better Children's Stories," *The Atlantic*, January 6, 2016, https://www.theatlantic .com/entertainment/archive/2016/01/why-the-british-tell-better -childrens-stories/422859/.

4. Eileen Kennedy-Moore, "A Simple Strategy to Help Worried Kids," *Growing Friendships* (blog), *Psychology Today*, June 23, 2017, https://www.psychologytoday.com/blog/growing-friendships /201706/simple-strategy-help-worried-kids.

5. Samantha Schmidt, "6-Year-Old Made $11 Million in One

Year Reviewing Toys on You Tube," *The Washington Post*, December 11, 2017, https://www.washingtonpost.com/news/morning-mix/wp/2017/12/11/6-year-old-made-11-million-in-one-year-reviewing-toys-on-you-tube.

6. "Alike Short Film," https://vimeo.com/194276412.

7. Ziauddin Yousafzai, "My Daughter, Malala," posted March 2014, https://www.ted.com/talks/ziauddin_yousafzai_my_daughter_malala.

CHAPTER 4

1. Robert Coles, "The Inner Lives of Children," interview by Krista Tippett, On Being Project, January 1, 2009, http://www.onbeing.org/program/inner-lives-children/transcript/1270.

2. Lisa Miller, *The Spiritual Child* (New York: St. Martin's Press, 2015), 12.

3. Miller, *Spiritual Child*, 43.

4. Monica Parker, *OMG! How Children See God* (Deerfield Beach, FL: Health Communications, 2016).

5. https://www.youtube.com/watch?v=e2w8Pczq7is.

6. Miller, *Spiritual Child*, 191.

7. Kerry Egan, "What People Talk about Before They Die," CNN, October 25, 2017, http://edition.cnn.com/2016/12/20/health/what-people-talk-about-before-dying-kerry-egan/index.html.

CHAPTER 5

1. Drew Hart, *Troubles I've Seen: Changing the Way the Church Views Racism* (Harrisonburg, VA: Herald, 2016), chapter 1, Kindle.

2. Morgan Lee, "Where John Piper and Other Evangelicals Stand on Black Lives Matter," *Christianity Today*, May 13, 2016, http://www.christianitytoday.com/gleanings/2016/may/where -john-piper-evangelicals-stand-black-lives-matter-blm.html.

3. Hart, *Troubles I've Seen*, chapter 4.

4. James Baldwin, "As Much Truth As One Can Bear," *New York Times Book Review*, January 14, 1962.

5. Ta-Nehesi Coates, *Between the World and Me* (New York: Spiegel & Grau, 2015), 108.

6. Po Bronson and Ashley Merryman, "Even Babies Discriminate: A Nurtureshock Excerpt," *Newsweek*, September 4, 2009, http://www.newsweek.com/even-babies-discriminate-nurture shock-excerpt-79233.

7. "Juvenile Incarceration Rates Are Down; Racial Disparities Rise," *Morning Edition*, NPR, January 2, 2015, https://www.npr.org /2015/01/02/374511130/juvenile-incarceration-rates-are-down-racial -disparities-rise-dramatically.

8. Hart, *Troubles I've Seen*, chapter 2.

9. Sharon Chang, *Raising Mixed Race: Multiracial Asian Children in a Post-Racial World* (New York: Routledge, 2016), chapter 1, Kindle.

10. Chang, *Raising Mixed Race*, chapter 1.

11. Chang, *Raising Mixed Race*, chapter 2.

12. Erin N. Winkler, "Children Are Not Colorblind: How Young Children Learn Race," *PACE* 3, no. 3 (2009): 1–8, https:// inclusions.org/wp-content/uploads/2017/11/Children-are-Not -Colorblind.pdf.

13. Banaji is quoted in Chang, *Raising Mixed Race*, chapter 3.

14. Chang, *Raising Mixed Race*, chapter 3.

15. Citron is quoted in Louise Derman-Sparks, Carol Tanaka Higa, and Bill Sparks, "Children, Race and Racism: How Race Awareness Develops," 3, https://www.teachingforchange.org/ wp-content/uploads/2012/08/ec_childrenraceracism_english.pdf.

16. Chang, *Raising Mixed Race*, chapter 8.

17. Christopher Myers, "The Apartheid of Children's Literature," *New York Times*, March 15, 2014, http://www.nytimes.com/2014/03/16/opinion/sunday/the-apartheid-of-childrens-literature.html. Also Daniel José Older, "Do Black Children's Lives Matter If Nobody Writes about Them?," *The Guardian*, November 6, 2015, http://www.theguardian.com/commentisfree/2015/nov/06/do-black-childrens-lives-matter-if-nobody-writes-about-them.

18. Valerie Strauss, "Just How Racist Is Children's Literature? The Author of 'Was the Cat in the Hat Black?' Explains," *Washington Post*, December 11, 2017, https://www.washingtonpost.com/news/answer-sheet/wp/2017/12/11/just-how-racist-is-childrens-literature-the-author-of-was-the-cat-in-the-hat-black-explains/?utm_term=.f0a0cbd50474.

19. https://www.embracerace.org.

20. http://www.teachingforchange.org.

21. Taryn Finley, "This 11-Year-Old Wants to Help Kids Discover Books They Can Relate To," *Huffington Post*, January 25, 2016, http://www.huffingtonpost.com/entry/this-11-year-old-wants-to-help-kids-discover-books-they-can-relate-to_us_56a65087e4b0404eb8f2438f.

22. "Ellen Meets a Little Literary Activist," http://ellentube.com/videos/0-vz3xp95j/.

23. Kenneth Braswell, *Daddy, There's a Noise Outside* (Atlanta: Black Rose Mediaworks, 2015).

24. Breanna Edwards, "Father Pens Book to Explain Protest to Kids in the Time of Black Lives Matter," The Root, February 7, 2016, https://www.theroot.com/father-pens-book-to-explain-protest-to-kids-in-the-time-1790854182.

CHAPTER 6

1. See her Ted Talk (https://www.ted.com/talks/chimamanda
_ngozi_adichie_we_should_all_be_feminists), which was later published as a book.

2. Mark Ruffalo (@MarkRuffalo), Twitter, February 24, 2018,
https://twitter.com/MarkRuffalo/status/967539333027770368.

3. See Cindy Brandt, "When Kristoff Asks Anna for Consent
in Frozen," *Unfundamentalist Parenting* (blog), May 16, 2016, http://
www.patheos.com/blogs/unfundamentalistparenting/2016/05/when
-kristoff-asks-anna-for-consent-in-frozen/.

4. See Rebecca J. Erickson, "Why Emotion Work Matters: Sex,
Gender, and the Division of Household Labor," *Journal of Marriage
and Family* 67, no. 2 (May 2005): 337–51.

5. Ryan Stollar, "Children, Disobey Your Parents in the Lord, for
This Is Right," Unfundamentalist Parenting (blog), May 9, 2016, http://
www.patheos.com/blogs/unfundamentalistparenting/2016/05
/children-disobey-your-parents-in-the-lord-for-this-is-right/.

6. Amanda Barbee, "Naked and Ashamed: Women and Evangelical Purity Culture," *The Other Journal Blog*, March 3, 2014,
https://theotherjournal.com/2014/03/03/naked-and-ashamed
-women-and-evangelical-purity-culture/.

CHAPTER 7

1. Joyce Ann Mercer, *Welcoming Children: A Practical Theology
of Childhood* (Atlanta: Chalice, 2005), chapter 3, Kindle.

2. Mercer, *Welcoming Children*, chapter 3.

3. Mercer, *Welcoming Children*, chapter 3.

4. Kim John Payne, *Simplicity Parenting* (New York: Ballantine
Books, 2009), chapter 3, Kindle.

5. Mercer, *Welcoming Children*, chapter 3.

6. David M. Csinos and Ivy Beckwith, *Children's Ministry in the Way of Jesus* (Downers Grove, IL: InterVarsity Press, 2013), 41.

7. See https://www.facebook.com/Greenchildmagazine/ and https://www.facebook.com/awilderchild/.

8. Naomi Klein, *This Changes Everything: Capitalism vs. the Climate* (New York: Simon & Schuster, 2014), chapter 1, Kindle.

9. *Unless We Act Now: The Impact of Climate Change on Children* (New York: UNICEF, 2015), 6, http://www.unicef.org/publications /files/Unless_we_act_now_The_impact_of_climate_change_on_children.pdf.

10. Andrea Germanos, "All Eyes on Oregon Courtroom Where It's 'Small Children vs Big Oil,'" Common Dreams, March 9, 2016, http://www.commondreams.org/news/2016/03/09/all-eyes-oregon -courtroom-where-its-small-children-vs-big-oil.

11. Cole Mellino, "Teens Sue Government for Failing to Address Climate Change for Future Generations," EcoWatch, February 23, 2015, https://www.ecowatch.com/teens-sue-government -for-failing-to-address-climate-change-for-future-1882012825.html.

12. See Elizabeth Svoboda, "America's Top 50 Green Cities," *Popular Science*, February 8, 2008, https://www.popsci.com /environment/article/2008-02/americas-50-greenest-cities.

13. See https://storyofstuff.org.

14. Klein, *This Changes Everything*, chapter 2.

CHAPTER 8

1. John Shore, "Southern Baptist Pastor Accepts Gay Son, Changes His Church," *John Shore* (blog), May 29, 2014, http://www .patheos.com/blogs/johnshore/2014/05/southern-baptist-pastor -accepts-his-gay-son-changes-his-church/.

2. Jonathan Merritt, "The Downfall of the Ex-Gay Movement," *Atlantic*, October 6, 2015, https://www.theatlantic.com/politics

/archive/2015/10/the-man-who-dismantled-the-ex-gay-ministry
/408970/.

3. Karen S. Peterson, "Report on Sex Prompts Call for Satcher's
Ouster," *USA Today*, June 29, 2001, http://usatoday30.usatoday.com
/news/health/2001-06-28-surgeon-general-sex.htm.

4. Deborah Jian Lee, *Rescuing Jesus: How People of Color, Women,
and Queer Christians are Reclaiming Evangelicalism* (Boston: Beacon,
2015), 154.

5. Victoria M. Massie, "LGBTQ Religion Activist: It's Time to
Talk about America's Faith-Based Homophobia Problem," *Vox*, June
15, 2016, http://www.vox.com/2016/6/15/11932454/orlando-shooting
-lgbtq-homophobia-religion.

6. Joani Lea Jack, "Unfolding Miracles: Human Sexuality," *Joa-
niLeaJack* (blog), February 7, 2016, http://www.joanileajack.com/
unfolding-miracles-human-sexuality/.

7. Michelle Ruiz, "Gays Against Guns: How the LGBT Community Is Rallying for Gun Control," *Vogue*, June 27, 2016, http://
www.vogue.com/13451637/lgbt-community-gun-control-after
-orlando-attack/.

8. Benjamin Moberg, "God and the 48%," *Registered Run-
away* (blog), May 28, 2015, http://runawaywrites.com/2015/05/28/
god-and-the-48/.

CHAPTER 9

1. "Connecting with Children by Connecting with Ourselves,"
video recording, https://drshefali.com/project/connecting-with
-children-by-connecting-with-ourselves/.

2. *A Book About Things I Will Tell My Daughter*, https://prod-
ucts.bottlecap.press/products/tell.

3. https://momsdemandaction.org.

4. https://www.facebook.com/permalink.php?story_fbid=3991 52997191006&id=100012889261389.

5. "Parkland Student Puts Lawmakers on Notice," https://www .facebook.com/YESSHECAN2018/videos/1871338679573971.

6. "Jason Reynolds—Serving Young Readers with 'Long Way Down,'" The Daily Show with Trevor Noah, January 23, 2018, http:// www.cc.com/video-clips/avk8pe/the-daily-show-with-trevor-noah -jason-reynolds---serving-young-readers-with--long-way-down-.